THE FOOD & COOKING OF
HUNGARY

THE FOOD & COOKING OF
HUNGARY

65 CLASSIC RECIPES FROM A GREAT TRADITION IN 300 PHOTOGRAPHS

SILVENA JOHAN LAUTA

WITH PHOTOGRAPHY BY TOBY SCOTT

aquamarine

This edition is published by Aquamarine, an imprint of Anness Publishing Ltd, Blaby Road, Wigston, Leicestershire LE18 4SE

info@anness.com;
www.aquamarinebooks.com;
www.annesspublishing.com

If you like the images in this book and would like to investigate using them for publishing, promotions or advertising, please visit our website www.practicalpictures.com for more information.

Publisher: Joanna Lorenz
Editorial director: Helen Sudell
Project editor: Emma Clegg
Designer: Simon Daley
Photography: Toby Scott
Home economist: Mari Williams
Prop stylist: Wei Tang
Production controller: Bessie Bai

ETHICAL TRADING POLICY

Jacket image: Oregano and Cumin Dumplings (see page 62) with Transylvanian Venison Stew (see pages 92–93).

PUBLISHER'S ACKNOWLEDGEMENTS

The publishers would like to thank the following for permission to reproduce their images: Alamy p6 Guy Harrop; p7tl funkyfood London, Paul Williams; p7tm Jon Arnold Images Ltd; p7tr E.D. Torial; p9b Nathan Benn; p10b Tierfotoagentur; p11t PjrTravel; p11b Adrian Sherratt; p12bl and p12br funkyfood London, Paul Williams; p13tr Chad Ehlers; p13b foodfolio; p14t funkyfood London, Paul Williams; p14 br Chris Fredriksson; p15bl foodfolio; p15br Guy Harrop; Bridgeman: p8bl Archives Charmet; p8br DHM; p9t Archives Charmet; Corbis p10t Paul Almasy; p13tl Austrian Archives; 14bl TBC; p15t Paul Almasy. t=top, b=bottom, r=right, l=left, m=middle.
All other photographs © Anness Publishing Ltd.

PUBLISHER'S NOTES

Although the advice and information in this book are believed to be accurate and true at the time of going to press, neither the author nor the publisher can accept any legal responsibility or liability for any errors or omissions that may be made, nor for any inaccuracies nor for any harm or injury that comes about from following instructions or advice in this book.

- Bracketed terms are intended for American readers.
- For all recipes, quantities are given in both metric and imperial measures and, where appropriate, in standard cups and spoons. Follow one set of measures, but not a mixture, because they are not interchangeable.
- Standard spoon and cup measures are level. 1 tsp = 5ml, 1 tbsp = 15ml, 1 cup = 250ml/8fl oz.
- Australian standard tablespoons are 20ml. Australian readers should use 3 tsp in place of 1 tbsp for measuring small quantities of gelatine, flour, salt, etc.
- American pints are 16fl oz/2 cups. American readers should use 20fl oz/2½ cups in place of 1 pint when measuring liquids.
- Electric oven temperatures in this book are for conventional ovens. When using a fan oven, the temperature will probably need to be reduced by about 10–20°C/20–40°F. Since ovens vary, you should check with your manufacturer's instruction book for guidance.
- The nutritional analysis given for each recipe is calculated per portion (i.e. serving or item), unless otherwise stated. If the recipe gives a range, such as Serves 4–6, then the nutritional analysis will be for the smaller portion size, i.e. 6 servings. Measurements for sodium do not include salt added to taste.
- Medium (US large) eggs are used unless otherwise stated.

Contents

Introduction

On the eastern side of Europe lies the small, landlocked country of Hungary. This flat, fertile region provides history and spectacle, from sleepy villages, baroque towns and medieval castles to the lively capital of Budapest, set in a landscape of rolling hills and a large freshwater lake. The shimmering surface of Lake Balaton reflects the sunlight to create a Mediterranean climate that benefits the surrounding vineyards. This has been the homeland of many, including the Romans and the Ottoman Turks, and has seen changing fortunes as invaders from east and west, north and south arrived, leaving their own stamp on the area's agriculture and cooking.

Character and food influences

The national characteristics of the Hungarian people have often been described as fiery and temperamental, just like their favourite culinary ingredient, paprika. A highly emotional and mercurial people, they are family oriented, always showing great respect for their elders and for Hungarian cultural heritage, which is unique in Europe – a true melting pot of influences from far and wide. Their wonderfully vibrant cuisine has flourished and developed throughout the years of occupation that have so often changed the fortunes of Hungary since Roman times.

Hungarians have a thirst for knowledge of all kinds. Their attitude toward foreign cultures, and foreign cuisine, has always been based on a sympathetic curiosity, never rejecting new tastes, but absorbing and adapting them with open-hearted generosity. As far back as the 9th century, the nomadic Magyar people who settled on the plains brought recipes for hearty and practical stews, making use of available meat and vegetables, as well as dried ingredients carefully prepared and saved for the lean months. The Italians who came to the Hungarian court in the 15th century imported onions and garlic; 150 years of the Ottoman Empire saw the first use of that essential Hungarian ingredient, paprika, as well as filo pastry and coffee; the Austrians passed on their love of cream, cakes and pastries; the Germans introduced sauerkraut and dumplings.

Hearty country fare

The cuisine of the Hungarian countryside remains much as it has been for centuries. In agricultural regions, innkeepers and private hosts still welcome their guests into a homely and cosy environment. The table is often laid with a home-made embroidered tablecloth, and groans with an array of traditional hearty fare in large portions. These recipes were developed as a midday meal that would sustain workers in the fields and warm them up in the freezing winter months. As a blueprint for solid sustenance to maintain energy throughout the day, a Hungarian lunch is hard to beat.

Soups are a vital element, a filling appetizer that starts the warming process, packed with vegetables or fruit and often topped with sour cream. Meat stews usually appear as the main course, with plenty of paprika to enliven the basic ingredients and bread to mop up the delicious gravy. Then there will be creamy, substantial desserts, pies, and puddings using local fruit and nuts.

LEFT Traditional Hungarian sausages for sale in the Vörösmarty Square Christmas Market in Budapest.

City influences

In Budapest and the other major cities, things are rather different. Foreign influences are once again flooding the streets, this time from all around the world. These include Italian, French, Spanish, Japanese and even Indian restaurants. Traditional Hungarian cuisine is still thriving in the capital, but it is changing as it has done throughout the centuries, adapting to fit modern expectations. Hungarians are beginning to demand lighter versions of their own cuisine, using vegetable oil rather than butter and lard, for example, and perhaps serving smaller portions for the deskbound workers of today.

There is so much delicious food to delight the visitor to Hungary. Whether you are eating in a new bar in Budapest, in an out-of-the-way village inn, or in a waterside restaurant overlooking Lake Balaton, the meal will be tasty, spicy, substantial and full of traditional ingredients.

How to use this book

The recipes in this volume give step-by-step instructions for making all the major dishes of present-day Hungarian cuisine, plus many traditional recipes passed down within families for special

RIGHT Hungary is mostly flat, rolling plains with some hills and low mountains.

occasions, such as Easter or Christmas. We start with soups, a strong presence in Hungarian meals. Next come appetizers, light dishes often based on cottage cheese, herbs and salad vegetables. Dumplings, pasta and pancakes have their own chapter as they are a vital part of most stews and soups; these are followed by a section on main course recipes, using fish, meat and game. Finally, the delights of Hungarian desserts and baking are described in mouthwatering detail. You will find a recipe here for every occasion, from a family meal to a gourmet dinner party, and many are sure to become favourites.

ABOVE FAR LEFT A Hungarian woman preparing dough for lepény, a shortcrust pastry made with butter, flour and eggs. Sweet and savoury fillings for lepény include plum, cherry, and curd cheese with dill.

ABOVE MIDDLE Gerbeaud Cukrászda, a famous traditional pastry shop and café in Budapest. Established by Henrik Kugler in 1858, it was expanded by its subsequent owner, Emil Gerbeaud.

ABOVE The Miró Café in the Castle District of Budapest is a popular tourist destination with its wrought-iron furniture and displays of local artwork and photography.

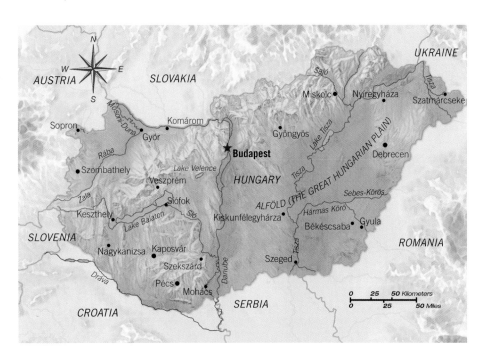

The roots of Hungarian cuisine

Hungary lies in a central position in Europe, between the huge bulk of Russia to the north and east and the smaller European countries such as Austria, Germany, and Italy to the south and west. For centuries, invaders have passed through or settled here, and every time people from these alien cultures decided to stay and put down roots, interesting new dishes and ingredients have arrived with them. From the poorest country cottage to the king's castle, these new influences have filtered through into the all-embracing Hungarian cuisine, and have been accepted and transformed by local cooks.

Arrival of the nomadic Magyars

When the first Magyars settled in the Carpathian basin in AD 895, they had already assimilated a rich mix of cultures and languages through their years of nomadic existence. They had travelled hundreds of miles from the Ural Mountains in present-day Russia, herding livestock but not settling to farm until they arrived on the fertile plains of Hungary. Meanwhile, the Magyars had learned to cook with whatever they could find, making one-pot stews cooked over an open fire. The Hungarian language dates back to these Magyar days, and has a common origin with that spoken in Finland, Estonia and parts of Russia.

The creation of the monarchy

At the end of the 3rd century AD, Grand Prince Géza and his son Stephen (István) founded a Christian ruling dynasty that was destined to last in some form for 946 years, despite many invasions and setbacks. This continuity of regal power helped to give Hungarians a real sense of national identity in their culture, as well as stability in their daily lives.

In early 1241, Mongol armies, led by the grandsons of Genghis Khan, rode into Hungary, and crushed the Hungarian army, destroying all before them. The Mongols left no food traditions behind; their rule was brutal and vicious, and the Hungarian nation's survival hung by a thread.

BELOW LEFT The Mongol Invasion of Hungary in 1241 during the reign of Béla IV (1206–70), King of Hungary and Croatia.

BELOW A woodcut of Matthias Corvinus of Hungary (1527), by Johannes Lichtenberger.

LEFT The Kuruc Uprising against the Habsburgs (1703–11, Hungarian School), saw the victory of Austrian and British forces against a French-Bavarian army.

But the descendants of the royal line were reinstated when, in the 15th century, Matthias Corvinus became king at just 15 years old. He was well educated, spoke numerous languages and was a patron of the arts. His rule was a time of affluence, and by the time he died, Hungary had become a great power in Europe. His third wife, Beatrice of Naples, had a huge influence on the development of Hungarian cuisine. She brought her native Mediterranean food culture with her to Budapest, with many new ingredients, including garlic, pasta and onions.

Foreign domination

After the death of Matthias Corvinus, Hungary went into a period of general decline, culminating in the invasion of the country by the Ottoman Turks and an occupation that lasted 150 years. The Turks had a huge and generally beneficial effect on Hungarian cookery, including the introduction of that typically Hungarian ingredient, paprika, as well as filo pastry, rice, stuffed (bell) peppers and aubergines (eggplants), corn, tomatoes, cherries and coffee.

The year 1697 brought the beginning of the collapse of the Ottoman empire and the rise of the Austrian Habsburgs. The best-known Austrian import was

RIGHT A Yom Kippur service in the Great Synagogue in Budapest.

that acquired taste, sauerkraut, plus elaborate desserts and creamy pastries. In 1867, the Austrian Habsburgs came to an agreement to share power with the Hungarian government and divided the former Austrian Empire between them. Hungary flourished. Hotels, restaurants and pastry shops sprang up, and the culinary arts, as well as music, fine art and architecture were in full flow throughout the end of the 19th century and the first half of the 20th century.

At this prosperous time, any Hungarian chef worth his salt went to study in France, and many brought the refined influence of French cooking back to their own country. One of the best known was József Marchal, who became chef to Napoleon III, and returned to Hungary to work at the Gundel restaurant, the most famous and elegant of all the Budapest restaurants.

Jewish dishes also became part of Hungarian cuisine at this time, as the Jewish population expanded in Budapest before the Second World War. One of the best-known is sólet, a slow-cooked dish of beans that was made in a special pot and sealed on Friday evening for eating warm on the Sabbath (Saturday). The variations on this dish are endless, but all agree that the addition of smoked and unsmoked meat is essential.

Surviving Soviet rule

As with so many European countries that came under Soviet influence, 40 years of communism after the Second World War did little for Hungarian cuisine – there was no option but to make the best of whatever food was available. Terrible economic stagnation led to chronic shortages and rationing of even the most basic foodstuffs. However, since 1991, Hungarian cuisine has once more been revived with renewed optimism, as it has so many times in the past.

The larder of Europe

This small, landlocked European country, which measures only 160 miles north to south and 320 miles east to west, once shared power with Austria as the joint head of an empire that ruled over most of central Europe. Its borders are now as they were set by the Treaty of Trianon, shortly after the First World War, following the collapse of the Habsburg empire. Despite its restricted size and its lack of coastline, Hungary has great potential as an agricultural producer, with a naturally fertile farming area in the central region where the level terrain and stable climate allow for mass production of crops.

Plains and waterways

The massive River Danube forms part of the northern border with Slovakia before turning south and traversing central Hungary, dividing the country and the capital city, Budapest, into two parts. Further east, Hungary's other major river, the Tisza, also flows from north to south. These two major waterways have created a level grassland between them with fertile

LEFT The Puszta, Alföld or Great Hungarian Plain, in the Bugac region, is an area of arid grasslands in Eastern Hungary.

BELOW Hungarian grey longhorn feeding on prairie land in the Puszta, once extensively used for cattle grazing.

soil, which is ideal for all kinds of agriculture, especially grain production and cattle farming.

The Great Hungarian Plain

The rolling plains of the Great Hungarian Plain, occupy more than half the agricultural land of Hungary. This vast and extremely fertile region has cold snowy winters and seemingly endless hours of sunshine in spring, summer and autumn. This area has become known as the larder of Hungary, and during the time of the Austro-Hungarian empire it provided food for much of Europe. The region is the home of traditional Magyar dishes such as goulash and stuffed cabbage.

The area between the Danube and Tisza rivers was once liable to flooding in the winter months, but the rivers have been tamed to irrigate the land. This area contains enormous poultry farms, including those rearing geese for the production of foie gras. Most of the meat, grain, fruit and vegetables that Hungary consumes also comes from here. Legend has it that this land is so fertile, if you plant a dry stick in the earth, it will burst into life.

The plains were once filled with cattle, vast herds that were driven hundreds of miles to the markets of Moravia (now the eastern Czech Republic), Austria, northern Italy and Germany. The origin of the word 'goulash' comes from the name for cattle herders, as the

Hungarian word 'gulyás' means 'herdsman'. The animals they kept were Hungarian Grey cattle, hardy creatures with huge horns, reared for beef. This ancient breed was gradually replaced by dairy cattle and the Hungarian Grey has now almost disappeared.

Rivers, hills and lakes

To the west of the Danube lies Transdanubia, an area of gently rolling countryside, valleys and hills, extending to the foothills of the Alps where Hungary borders Austria. In the centre lies spectacular Lake Balaton, nearly 80 kilometers (fifty miles) long and 16 kilometers (ten miles) wide. The largest lake in central Europe, many resorts and spas are dotted around its shores.

It is also a productive fishing area, even though the waters are only about three metres (10 feet) deep. There are plenty of freshwater fish such as eels and pike, and above all zander, which is closely related to perch. Many of the waterside restaurants lining the shores of the lake serve this fish with a traditional side dish of corn on the cob.

As the lake area receives a fair amount of rain but also warm summer and autumn sunshine, vineyards have sprung up on the slopes of the surrounding hills. These grapes make high-quality, fruity wines.

The Little Hungarian Plain

Close to the foothills of the Austrian Alps in the north-west corner of Transdanubia is a pleasant agricultural area known as the Kisalföld, the Little Hungarian Plain, with the Danube running through it from west to east. It is famed for its

ABOVE View of the River Danube and the Hungarian Parliament in Budapest.

indigenous produce such as chestnuts, which the locals use for both savoury and sweet recipes. Here too, some of the best wild mushrooms are to be found in autumn. The lovely countryside and fresh air have always attracted the aristocracy, and many, such as the renowned Esterhazy family, built their spectacular mansions here.

Thermal springs

Hungary is particularly rich in thermal waters, with more than a hundred spa resorts dotted around the country, all sourcing from the Danube; Budapest is known as the world's spa capital. Some of the baths date right back to the Ottoman empire in the 18th century, and are spectacularly beautiful buildings. The thermal waters, which are rich in minerals, can be drunk or used for bathing, and many believe that they have a beneficial effect on some medical conditions.

Tastes of Hungary

This small country in the heart of Europe treasures its reputation as a food-lover's paradise. Throughout the years of foreign domination, whether by Mongols, Turks, Austrians or Soviet Russians, Hungarians have preserved their favourite dishes and passed them down from one generation to the next. The generosity of spirit of the Magyar people, the original Hungarian tribe, spills over into the size of their meals, which can be rather overwhelming for the unwary visitor. A good lunch always consists of at least three courses, and needs to be followed by an hour's rest to aid digestion.

The Magyar cooking pot

The nomadic tribes of ancient Hungary were, by their very nature, always on the move, herding their animals to new grazing pastures. This meant that meals had to be cooked in one large, practical cooking pot over an open fire, using dried, cubed beef as the base and cooking it slowly in its own juices to release all the flavour. Many of the most authentic dishes of Hungary were originally made in this way, and it is still a tradition in country areas for the man of the house to take charge of the outdoor cooking pot, making a delicious beef goulash (more of a soup than a stew) for everyone to share at parties and family celebrations. Otherwise the family kitchen has generally become the woman's domain for the preparation of everyday meals.

Paprika and coffee

Hungarian cooks gladly adapted the recipes brought to their country by Turks and Austrians between the late 16th century and the early 19th century. It is amazing to think that paprika, the warming red chilli spice so beloved of the Turks, was previously unknown in Hungary – it is now used every day in the Hungarian kitchen. There are various types of paprika, but two main forms: the delicate red one, which is added to soups and stews at the beginning of the cooking process and permeates the dish with its sweetish aroma; and the fierce orange-brown one, which is generally added at the end of the cooking process to give the dish a fiery kick. The recipes here all use sweet paprika, the more delicate form.

BELOW LEFT Beef pörkölt (marhapörkölt) being cooked in a large pan at the Paprika Food Festival in Kalocsa.

BELOW Chilli peppers (*Capsicum annum*) drying in the sun, in preparation for making Hungarian paprika.

Coffee is another Turkish import that has become a staple of the food culture. Hungarians tend not to drink much tea, but do enjoy a cup of hot chocolate instead of coffee from time to time, maybe accompanied by a rich creamy cake in the Austrian style, or a piece of fruit strudel wrapped in delicate Turkish filo pastry.

The daily diet
The majority of Hungarians eat three good meals a day, starting with a substantial breakfast. This can include fresh seeded bread or pastries with butter, jam and honey, or cold sliced meat, cheese and salads of fresh tomatoes, (bell) peppers, cucumber and radishes. Strong coffee is the favourite breakfast drink to get the body and brain into gear.

Lunchtime brings the main meal of the day, and the break from work will often last as long as two hours – plenty of time for a three-course meal followed by a short nap. Soup is usually the first course, and next comes a meat dish with a side salad or pickled vegetables. Cake, strudel or sweet pancakes follow, and the meal ends with whichever fruit happens to be in season.

The evening meal is taken at about eight, and tends to be the lightest meal of the day. In summer, charcuterie with seasonal vegetables such as tomatoes, peppers and cucumber is the preference, but in winter, hearty stews feature more often than cold meat.

Goulash, the classic dish
This tasty, paprika-flavoured beef soup has been very important to Hungarians for centuries. During the years of Austro-Hungarian rule, everything German was seen as desirable, while traditional Hungarian dishes, costumes, dance and even language were discouraged. Luckily, no discouragement could stop the people from making their favourite goulash every day. The recipe survived, and eventually it was even taken abroad by such eminent chefs as Georges Auguste Escoffier (1846–1935), who served a typical Hungarian goulash to his rich clients in the Grand Hotel, Monte Carlo.

ABOVE LEFT A Hungarian coffee house photographed circa 1900.

ABOVE RIGHT Nuts, gourds, peppers and paprika at the Great Market Hall, Budapest.

The market in Budapest
Budapest, the Hungarian capital, home to almost two million people, was created when the historic towns of Buda, on the west bank, and Pest, the commercial centre on the east bank, were united in 1873. The 'big market', as locals call it, or Market Hall No.1 as it is officially known, first opened in 1897. It was refurbished in the 1990s, and thrives despite the international competition from supermarkets. It contains everything that the countryside has to offer, with fruit, vegetables, cheese, fish, meat, poultry and tourist wares. It is also a popular meeting place, especially among the younger generations.

Feast days and festivals

There is nothing Hungarians enjoy more than a good celebration involving food, dancing, drinking and music. Apart from those that follow the religious calendar, there are a number of food festivals throughout the year; while the biggest and most elaborate ones are held in Budapest, which also calls itself "festival city", there are plenty of other events celebrating specific foods, spirits and wine all around Hungary. They are well worth seeking out for their vibrant, friendly atmosphere and abundance of local produce, as well as the delights of watching a dancing competition, listening to a display of baroque music or sampling a pig roast.

ABOVE Man in traditional dress at the annual wine festival in Badacsony, a scenic wine region near Lake Balaton.

New Year

After the traditional Hungarian Christmas, which is a time for families and quiet contemplation, New Year's Eve is one big party. Parties are not confined to the home either, as all the clubs and restaurants are open and do an enormous amount of business. As the clock strikes midnight, there is a moment of silence and remembrance, followed by a raucous rendition of the national anthem and toasts for a happy and prosperous new year.

The Hungarians generally welcome in the new year with sparkling wine, which is sold by the glass from street stalls. Traditionally, pork brawn and roasted suckling pig with cabbage are the favourite dishes, or sausages with mustard or horseradish, bought from a stall and eaten in the street. Afterwards, a bowl of cabbage soup is vital to ward off a hangover. It is customary to eat frugal lentils on New Year's Day, showing that careful housekeeping will see the family through the coming year.

Spring festivals

Two food festivals in the dark days of February, just as the year turns towards spring, demonstrate typical country traditions. The first is in honour of the mangalica, a rare breed of furry pig native to Hungary. The best live mangalica pigs are on show in Budapest, alongside stalls selling everything to do with pigs and pork.

The second February festival is celebrated in the village of Szatmárcseke, 300 miles east of Budapest on the border with Ukraine. This event focuses on a dumpling called cinke, made with flour and potatoes, a staple food in rural areas when meat was scarce. Shaped like tiny birds, these are fried and served with

BELOW LEFT A chef at the Mangalica Festival in Budapest, where various dishes are made from mangalica pig meat.

BELOW A young girl in traditional dress painting Easter eggs, an ancient custom that is still popular today.

cottage cheese. Cinke are a main attraction on street stalls, along with plum jam, cakes, biscuits and bread. Everything is washed down with a strong spirit, palinka, made with plums or prunes, and there is dancing and singing.

Easter

Christianity may be less dominant in Hungary than it once was, but children and adults still paint eggs as they have done for centuries. On Easter Sunday morning, little children find small gifts beside their beds, and everyone eats a breakfast of eggs, ham and kalács, a special bread that is twisted into a braid.

Summer festivals

In May a four-day pálinka festival celebrates the varieties of fruit brandy. There are competitions for the best spirits, many distilled locally. June and September bring wine festivals all around the country, where there is also an array of delicious local food, particularly pork products.

Christmas

Hungarians decorate their Christmas trees not just with baubles and chocolates, but also with szaloncukor, sugary sweets wrapped in white tissue

The wedding feast

Weddings are a cause for great celebration in Hungary, with a large gathering of friends and family. The food served at the wedding breakfast varies from region to region, but what they have in common is quantity, with the table laden to breaking point. The feast usually begins with a meat soup containing little curls of pasta known as 'snails', which are made by the friends of the bride. This is often followed by paprika chicken with stuffed cabbage, then by pastries, a host of desserts and many wedding cakes contributed by the guests.

paper and brightly coloured foil. These used to be made from plain fondant, but now come in various forms, covered in chocolate or filled with marzipan.

The Christmas holiday is a quiet celebration for families and close friends. Christmas Eve is the most important day, with presents for everyone and a wonderful feast in the evening. Meat soup is followed by turkey with chestnut stuffing or roast pork with vegetables, and the meal ends with a dessert made from poppy

seeds (a symbol of fertility). Some Hungarians still hold to the old tradition of serving fish on Christmas Eve, and eat breaded fillets of carp or fish soup instead of meat.

BELOW LEFT A street vendor prepares kürtos kalács, a sweet pastry baked on a cylindrical spit, for a Christmas market.

BELOW The Christmas market in Vörösmarty Square in Budapest offers traditional crafts as well as food specialities.

The Hungarian kitchen

Mention Hungarian cooking, and most people will think of that tasty paprika-flavoured dish, goulash. It is indeed the most common dish made in Hungary, although it is thought of as a soup rather than a main course, but there are plenty of other favourites that use all kinds of local produce, including freshwater fish, vegetables, fruit and herbs. The most important factor in Hungarian cuisine is the way that cooks have embraced imported ingredients such as paprika, coffee, tomatoes, onions and filo pastry over the centuries, so that they have become an essential part of the Hungarian diet.

Meat, fish and game

Beef, pork and veal are the most popular meats in Hungary, and feature on every dining table in this predominantly meat-eating country. The open plains of central Hungary are ideal for rearing beef cattle, and pigs have been raised here since Roman times. Many rural people still keep a family pig, which is destined for hams and sausages to feed the family throughout the winter. Veal is also cooked throughout Hungary, either fried simply as an escalope with a sour cream sauce, or ground to make tasty little croquettes.

People still come from all over Europe to hunt wild boar and deer in the sparsely populated countryside. There is plenty of space for wild animals to roam at will, particularly in the hills and forests in the west of the country. Venison makes a wonderful roast or braised dish, and it frequently features as a centrepiece for family celebrations. Local people also catch hare, rabbits and pheasants, and these are cooked in delicious recipes such as fricassee of rabbit with prunes.

As Hungary has no sea coast, fresh seafish is a rarity. However, there are plenty of carp, trout, salmon, eels and pike in the rivers and lakes; these are generally cooked very simply, with a tasty sauce.

Vegetables

The humble onion is the basic ingredient in many dishes. Chopped, it imparts flavour to goulash and pörkölt stew, or it can be left whole in soups. Until recently, onions were sometimes eaten raw, along with bread and bacon, for breakfast in rural communities.

Hungarians love tomatoes. The word for 'tomato' and for 'paradise' is the same: paradicsom. Large tomatoes with thin skins are used for cooking, and the smaller, more decorative ones for salads. Gardeners often preserve their tomatoes for winter by making them into a mouthwatering bottled tomato sauce.

Mushrooms are found in the woods and fields in autumn, and the big flat ones (portobello) make a convincingly meaty base for dishes such as Transylvanian stuffed mushrooms. Smaller button mushrooms are a tasty addition to creamy sauces and soups.

BELOW, FROM LEFT TO RIGHT Beef is the primary choice for meat dishes and is often used for specialities such as salami and ham; tomatoes and onions are invariably used as the foundation for vegetable and meat-based dishes; mushrooms are grown widely and used frequently in Hungarian cuisine.

Cabbage is another staple vegetable, and one that has been cultivated for centuries. It is eaten in stews, pickled or stuffed. Many Hungarians, including those that live in the cities, still make their own sauerkraut, a recipe brought to the country by Austrian cooks during the Austro-Hungarian empire.

Fruit

All kinds of fruits, particularly stone fruits such as plums, cherries and apricots, flourish in the warm summer climate. They are eaten fresh or in baked desserts and cakes, and made into winter preserves. The classic strudel contains layered apples, pears or cherries, often studded with dried fruit.

Fruit soups are an interesting speciality, often eaten chilled during hot weather as a refreshing appetizer. Sharp berries and cherries make the best fruit soups, with a piquant taste. Orchard fruits such as apples or pears can be blended with savoury ingredients and nuts, as in Kohlrabi, Apple and Almond Soup, giving the dish an aromatic flavour.

Many different fruits, including plums and cherries, are distilled into a strongly alcoholic spirit called pálinka, a real warmer in the bitter winter weather.

Nuts and seeds

Hungarian patisserie relies heavily on fragrant nuts. They are used whole, crushed, ground or made into pastes in cakes, strudels and cookies, adding wonderful flavour and texture.

ABOVE, FROM LEFT TO RIGHT Stone fruits, such as peaches, plums and cherries, thrive in the warm climate and feature in many classic dishes; nuts grown in Hungary include almonds and cashews; chestnuts are used to make a purée that appears in both savoury meat dishes and sweet desserts.

Almonds are delicately flavoured and enormously versatile. Fresh almonds are far more creamy and delicious than packaged ones, and they are good for you, being high in monounsaturated fat. Walnuts and pecans come to the fore in December, hence their use in festive cakes and puddings for Christmas.

Sweet chestnuts only grow in the northern parts of the Transdanubia region, where the nearby mountains provide the right kind of micro-climate for the trees. Not so many years ago, there were dozens of chestnut sellers to be seen in Budapest in winter, roasting the nuts over braziers in the streets for sale by the bag, but this tradition has sadly almost died out. Chestnut products such as purée are still used for savoury stuffings or sweet cakes, or combined with chocolate or cream and sour cherries as a dessert.

Poppy seeds are an ancient central European foodstuff, used in cooking for over 5000 years. In Hungary, blue-black poppy seeds are used for flavouring in bread and cakes, or sprinkled on top as a decoration.

Preparing sauerkraut

The most famous Hungarian sauerkraut is produced in the little town of Vecsés, just outside Budapest. Here, almost the entire town makes a living from producing sauerkraut and other pickled vegetables. Here is a basic recipe so that you can make your own.

1 Discard the outside leaves and stalk of a cabbage, then shred the inner leaves.

2 Make layers of cabbage in a large jar or crock, interspersed with salt, bay leaves, peppercorns, chillies and caraway seeds.

3 Press a weight on top and cover loosely. Store in a cool place and leave to ferment. The lactic acid produced during fermentation gives the sauerkraut its typical sour flavour.

Spices and herbs

The favourite spice of Hungary is paprika, introduced by the Ottoman Turks in the latter part of the 16th century. Initially it was not used in food at all, but was a decorative plant in flower gardens, carefully guarded by the Turks from the native people. It was the shepherds and herdsmen who had most contact with the Turkish invaders, and who started to add paprika to their meals. By the end of the 19th century, paprika had become the dominant spice in Hungarian cuisine.

In the days before mechanization, farmers would hang the picked peppers in the sun and then put them into earthenware ovens to dry further. The dry pods were crushed and the veins and seeds removed, then the flesh was ground into powder using a mortar and pestle. Paprika ranges from sweet to fiery hot, depending on the type of pepper from which it is produced. The hottest paprika does not come from bright red peppers, as you might think, but from orange-coloured ones. There are up to eight grades of paprika available in Hungary, but the one used in this book is sweet paprika, also called noble sweet paprika, a mild grade and the most commonly available.

To enjoy the full flavour and aroma of paprika it should be added to hot oil, but as it burns very easily, it is best to remove the pan from the heat while adding the spice and stir continuously. Burnt paprika tastes bitter, and will ruin a dish. Its full flavour does not last long in storage, so buy it in small quantities and store it in a cool place.

Other strong flavours often used in Hungarian stocks or sauces are horseradish, mustard and garlic, which bring out the flavour of many a fish or meat dish. Aromatic seeds and berries such as nutmeg, caraway and juniper are used to season vegetable, fish and meat dishes by adding them to a soup stock or marinade.

Garden herbs also feature strongly in Hungarian cuisine. Dill blends beautifully with freshwater fish such as pike, while parsley garnishes everything from the most delicate soup to a creamy chicken casserole. All the well-known herbs are found in these recipes, such as thyme, sage, oregano, basil, chives and mint. They can even form a side dish in themselves, as in the recipe for Herb and Cheese Fritters, where balls of feta cheese mixture are fried until crisp and laid on top of the leafy herb salad.

Pasta and dumplings

Almost as important to Hungarians as it is to Italians, pasta is used as an ingredient in savoury and sweet dishes. In the days when meat was not eaten on Fridays for religious reasons, pasta took over as the basis of a good meal with cheese or fish. There is an unwritten rule in Hungary that every dish must have its own particular shape of pasta: strawberry leaf-shaped pasta for use in

ABOVE, FROM LEFT TO RIGHT A spice introduced by the Ottoman Turks, paprika is made from the grinding of bell peppers or chillies; caraway, nutmeg and juniper are used individually as aromatic additions to stocks and marinades for savoury dishes; filo pastry was traditionally made by hand, but is now mostly bought ready made.

soups and stews; large squares for baked meat dishes; and long, flat ribbons with sugar, lemon rind and poppy seeds as a dessert.

Dumplings are a filling favourite, and can be sweet or savoury. Indeed, some are similar to Italian ravioli, with a tasty filling concealed inside, while herb or plain dumplings are simmered in stock and added to the meat dish on serving. Pancakes come in all kinds of flavours, with the basic pancake wrapped around savoury or sweet variations such as wild mushroom, feta cheese and garlic, or poppy seeds with vanilla.

Pastry and cakes

Although the recipes for many Hungarian cakes and pastries were imported from Austria during the 19th century, the basis for the popular dessert, fruit strudel, is filo pastry, a Turkish speciality. Every pastry shop has its own range of strudels, which can be served with coffee or hot chocolate, or to round off a meal. Filo pastry is very delicate and quite tricky to make, so most cooks buy it fresh or frozen from the supermarket.

Apricots, cherries, plums and pears are picked in summer and then preserved in syrup, to be used as the delicious base for a pie in the winter months. The topping is typically made of buttery pastry enlivened with sour cream for an extra depth of richness.

Dried fruit such as sultanas (golden raisins) and raisins often form part of a strudel filling, but these sweet fruits come into their own in the traditional Christmas loaf. Made of sweetened shortcrust pastry, this has a spicy fruit and nut filling and a citrus tang.

Dairy and eggs

Hungarians tend not to drink much fresh milk – they rarely add it to a hot drink such as tea or coffee. The dairy products they really love are sour cream and piquant cheeses such as feta cheese, goat's cheese, quark (curd cheese) and, above all, cottage cheese. Sour cream is often used for thickening sauces and soups, or adding to the popular Hungarian paprika-flavoured chicken dish, papricas. Cottage cheese makes a delicious dip when blended with the ubiquitous paprika, or a topping for dumplings and pancakes. Hungarian cheeses tend to be pale, soft and sharp, such as feta or ricotta, or the more solid Trappista, a traditional semi-soft cheese originally made in the monasteries of France.

Eggs are often served hard-boiled and sliced as part of a buffet salad, or finely chopped in mayonnaise dressing.

They are also used as a cooking ingredient in the wonderful range of gooey cakes and desserts.

Alcoholic drinks

The hilly south-facing slopes of Transdanubia are ideally sited for vineyards, and several varieties of grape have dotted the landscape here since Roman times. The best-known red wine is Egri Bikavér (Bull's Blood), and another well-known variety is Tokaji (Tokay), a sweet dessert wine with a strong, syrupy flavour. Tokaji is expensive, but a lightly chilled glass at the end of a meal with blue cheese or chocolate cake is not to be missed.

Though Hungarians enjoy a glass of wine, they are also partial to a drop of strong spirit, and their preference is for pálinka. This drink, which has been made for more than 500 years, is brandy distilled from fruit. To be recognized as genuine, the fruit must have been distilled in Hungary and the brandy an alcoholic content of at least 37.5%. It was once thought to aid digestion, particularly when the meal contains a lot of fatty, rich food.

Beer is the favoured beverage for outdoor celebrations. Local Hungarian beers are still widely produced, despite competition from international brewers, and a number of micro-breweries have sprung up in the last ten years or so. Most of these produce pale, lager-type beers that are served cold, and are refreshing on a hot day.

Coffee

Apart from favourite alcoholic beverages, the national drink of Hungary is, without doubt, coffee. The Turks brought coffee to Hungary in the latter part of the 16th century, when the strong, syrupy drink was known by the locals as "black soup". Budapest in the 19th and early 20th century was filled with wonderfully ornate coffee houses, places of important social interaction, with large windows that looked out on to the passing world. These cafés almost never closed, allowing the patrons to spend as much time as they liked over a coffee and a cake, reading the papers, playing chess or swapping the latest news with friends and neighbours. At lunch and dinner, full meals were served, and in the evening there was usually musical entertainment of some kind. Most of these great coffee houses were destroyed in the two world wars, although some have been renovated, such as Café Gerbeaud in Budapest. However, the taste for strong, sweet black coffee is unwavering and it remains an essential daily drink for most Hungarians.

BELOW, FROM LEFT TO RIGHT Dried fruit appears in desserts and cakes, and raisins and sultanas (golden raisins) are associated with fruit strudels; cottage, ricotta and goat's cheese are often components of traditional dishes; Hungarians adore coffee, which continues to typify the experience of modern Hungary.

SOUPS

Most Hungarians eat soup every single day – in fact, they are convinced that it is vital to promote good digestive health. No wonder there are hundreds of delicious soup recipes in Hungary, using many different ingredients based on whatever is available throughout the seasons. Soup is almost always served as the first course for lunch, a substantial and nutritious way to start a proper Hungarian meal. The lighter meal of the day tends to be served in the evening, and sometimes soup can stand on its own as the main course for dinner, simply accompanied by bread and fruit or cheese.

Rich and flavoursome to cool and sweet

Perhaps the most famous Hungarian soup is goulash, a delicious mixture full of succulent beef and tender vegetables. It was invented centuries ago by Magyar tribesmen, who carried dried beef cubes with them on their long treks across the plains and mountains, ready to simmer with spring water, herbs, spices and vegetables for a nourishing one-pot meal. These days goulash is seasoned with sweet paprika, and the vegetables are usually red (bell) peppers, potatoes and tomatoes. The final touch is a handful of tiny plain dumplings, galuska, which have been simmered separately in stock until they are light and fluffy and then added to the goulash. The distinctive rich, sweet flavour of goulash is the epitome of Hungarian cuisine.

There are many more favourite soup recipes in Hungary. A good ham hock or pieces of smoked bacon are simmered gently in broth with vegetables or pulses for a warming winter soup that is full of goodness. Pulses and grains blend particularly well with the strong flavours of ham, bacon, sausage, field (portabello) mushrooms and even sauerkraut.

Soup recipes are one of the few sources of vegetarian food in Hungary. There are plenty of nutritious vegetable dishes in this chapter, so the vegetarian diner will not feel deprived. These are based on garden and field ingredients such as mushrooms, kohlrabi, sorrel or cabbage. They can also contain dried pulses and grains such as pearl barley. With the addition of dumplings or tiny pasta shapes, these soups are filling enough to make a main meal.

Hungarian cooks have also devised plenty of refreshing chilled soups to allay the heat of summer. Not only do Hungarians enjoy savoury vegetable concoctions, they also delight in sharp fruit soups such as strawberry, gooseberry and cherry. Sweeter fruits such as strawberries can be made more piquant with buttermilk, sour cream and lemon juice. Cherries, gooseberries and blackcurrants have their own sharp flavour that cuts through to wake up the taste buds.

There is also a selection of fragrant sweet fruit soups, such as pear or apple, where the fruit is cooked and mixed with grated citrus rind, brown sugar and cinnamon or mixed (apple pie) spice for a luscious flavour.

Serves 6

450g/1lb/4 cups fresh ripe strawberries,
  hulled
150ml/¼ pint/⅔ cup buttermilk
250ml/8fl oz/1 cup sour cream
30ml/2 tbsp fresh lemon juice,
  if needed

Chilled Strawberry Soup
Hideg eperleves

This is a typical Hungarian fruit soup, made with fresh and delicious strawberries when
in season. If you happen to be lucky enough to taste a chilled fruit soup while visiting
Hungary, then you may stumble upon a wild strawberry or wild blueberry soup, which are
truly wonderful and have exceptionally delicate tart flavours. Blackcurrants, peaches and
cherries can also be used to make cooling summer soups.

1 Put the strawberries in a food
processor or blender and purée until
smooth.

2 Press through a sieve (strainer) and
stir in the buttermilk and sour cream.

3 Taste and, if you like, add a little
lemon juice for a slightly sourer
taste. Chill before serving.

COOK'S TIPS
• When choosing strawberries, the ones
with the most flavour have bright red
berries and green (not brown) caps.
Generally, a smaller size of berry will
be sweeter.
• Strawberries should be eaten as fresh
as possible. Do not wash them until you
are ready to consume them.
• Strawberries don't store well but they
can be frozen. Wash them, dry them and
remove the caps. Then put them on a
baking sheet and freeze. Place in a plastic
bag, remove the air and seal. You can keep
them in the freezer for up to 6 months.

PER SERVING: Energy 115kcal/478kJ; Protein 3g; Carbohydrate 7g, of which sugars 7g; Fat 8g, of which saturates 5g; Cholesterol 26mg; Calcium 81mg; Fibre 1.5g; Sodium 36mg

Serves 6
700g/1¾lb morello or sour cherries,
   stoned
1.5ml/¼ tsp mixed (apple pie) spice
juice and zest of 1 lemon
1 litre/1¾ pints water
75ml/5 tbsp caster (superfine) sugar
1 large egg yolk
250ml/8fl oz/1 cup sour cream
6–7 mint sprigs, leaves only, to serve
10ml/2 tbsp ground pistachios, to serve

Morello Cherry Soup
Hideg meggyleves

Soups made from seasonal fruits are a favourite central European treat, and cherry soup is one of the glories of the Hungarian table. It is associated with Shavuot, an ancient Jewish agricultural festival where an offering of the first fruit harvest was presented to Jehovah at the end of Passover. At this time dairy foods were feasted upon, with this dish often eaten at the start of a meal. It is delicious served with an extra spoonful or two of sour cream.

1 Trim the cherries and wash them well. Place in a large pan with the mixed spice, lemon juice and zest. Cover with the water and add the sugar.

2 Bring to simmer and cook for 10 minutes. Remove about half of the cherries, using a slotted spoon. Use a food processor to process the mixture until you get a smooth purée. Return to the soup and bring to boil.

3 Place the egg yolk and sour cream in a bowl and mix to combine. Add a cup of the cherry soup into the egg mixture and stir to mix well. Return the mixture to the rest of the soup.

4 Allow to simmer very gently for 2–3 minutes and remove from heat. Serve with mint and pistachios on top.

COOK'S TIP
For maximum flavour use cherries that have a bright, shiny and firm (but not hard) flesh. The darker the flesh, the sweeter the taste.

PER SERVING: Energy 212kcal/889kJ; Protein 3g; Carbohydrate 28g, of which sugars 28g; Fat 10g, of which saturates 6g; Cholesterol 62mg; Calcium 63mg; Fibre 1.8g; Sodium 30mg

Serves 6
600g/1lb 6oz ripe pears
grated rind of 1 orange
1.5ml/¼ tsp mixed (apple pie) spice
45ml/3 tbsp soft light brown sugar
45ml/3 tbsp cornflour (cornstarch)
250ml/8fl oz/1 cup sour cream

Chilled Pear Soup
Hideg körteleves

This light and slightly spiced soup made with ripe pears is an exotic choice as a light appetizer, a refreshing summer meal served with fresh rolls, or a deliciously sweet conclusion to a meal. It is an excellent option for a vegetarian, low-fat food choice. The soup can also be made with apples or plums.

1 Peel and core the pears, then slice thinly. Put the pears and 1.5 litres/ 2½ pints/6¼ cups water in a pan over medium heat. Add the orange rind, mixed spice and sugar. Stir in well and cook until the pears are soft.

2 Put the cornflour in a small bowl and stir in 60–75ml/4–5 tbsp water to blend to a smooth paste. Add the sour cream and stir to combine.

3 Add the sour cream mixture to the pear soup, then transfer to a food processor or blender and process until smooth and creamy. Chill and serve.

COOK'S TIPS
• Check the ripeness of pears by pressing the top of the fruit near the stem – it needs to be firm with a touch of give.
• To ripen pears at home, put the fruit in a paper bag with an air hole and keep at room temperature until they are just ripe.
• Pears become overripe very quickly – then the flesh becomes pulpy and loses its smoothness.

PER SERVING: Energy 182kcal/760kJ; Protein 2g; Carbohydrate 26g, of which sugars 19g; Fat 8g, of which saturates 5g; Cholesterol 25mg; Calcium 55mg; Fibre 1.6g; Sodium 24mg

Serves 6
450g/1lb/4 cups gooseberries, trimmed
60ml/4 tbsp caster (superfine) sugar
juice and grated rind of 1 small lemon
100ml/3½fl oz/½ cup sweet white wine
15ml/1 tbsp cornflour (cornstarch)
60ml/4 tbsp sour cream
a handful of blackberries, to serve

Chilled Gooseberry Soup with Blackberries
Hideg egresleves szederrel

This cooling summer soup is made with fresh gooseberries and sweet wine. Gooseberries are a valuable source of fibre and vitamins A and C. As well as being a tasty appetizer, the soup can also be paired with boiled meat or meat patties as a main meal. If you can get hold of the sweet, aromatic wine, Tokay, then this soup is just amazing.

1 Put the gooseberries in a large pan with the sugar. Add the lemon rind and juice with 1 litre/1¾ pints/4 cups water and the wine. Bring to the boil over medium heat and simmer for 20–25 minutes, or until the gooseberries are soft.

2 In a small bowl, mix the cornflour with the sour cream until smooth. Gradually add about 200ml/7floz/ scant 1 cup of the hot cooking liquid, stirring to make a smooth and creamy consistency.

3 Stir into the gooseberry mixture in the pan, add the wine and mix well to combine. Cook for 2 minutes, then cool and chill completely before serving. Serve cold, topped with fresh blackberries.

COOK'S TIPS
• Small green cooking gooseberries are available early in the season – they should have a firm and smooth flesh. Dessert gooseberries are available later in the season – these are sweeter.
• Adjust the quantities of sugar, according to your preference.

PER SERVING: Energy 118kcal/499kJ; Protein 1g; Carbohydrate 22g, of which sugars 20g; Fat 2g, of which saturates 1g; Cholesterol 6mg; Calcium 33mg; Fibre 3.2g; Sodium 9mg

Serves 6

1.2 litres/2 pints/5 cups chicken stock
4 kohlrabi, peeled and chopped
2 tart apples, peeled, cored and
chopped
4 parsley sprigs, leaves finely chopped
1.5ml/¼ tsp grated nutmeg
115g/4oz ground almonds
100ml/3½fl oz/scant ½ cup sour cream
15ml/1 tbsp lightly toasted flaked
(sliced) almonds
salt and ground black pepper

Kohlrabi, Apple and Almond Soup
Karalábéleves kertész módra

The typical Eastern European vegetable kohlrabi is used widely in the Hungarian kitchen
for making soups, stews or side dishes. Here is a light and incredibly easy soup to make,
thickened and given richness by ground almonds.

1 Put the chicken stock in a large
pan and add the chopped kohlrabi
and apples. Season to taste with salt
and pepper, and bring to the boil.
Reduce to a simmer and cook for 20
minutes, or until the kohlrabi and
apples are soft.

2 Add the parsley and adjust the
seasoning, then stir in the nutmeg.
Put the soup into a food processor or
blender and process until smooth
and creamy.

3 Add the ground almonds, then
return to the pan and simmer for
5 minutes more.

4 Serve the soup hot with a dollop of
sour cream on top, sprinkled with a
few toasted flaked almonds.

COOK'S TIP
Kohlrabi bulbs are available in white and
purple. The white ones have more flavour
when they are small.

PER SERVING: Energy 208kcal/865kJ; Protein 7g; Carbohydrate 9g, of which sugars 9g; Fat 16g, of which saturates 3g; Cholesterol 10mg; Calcium 102mg; Fibre 3.6g; Sodium 461mg

Serves 6
30g/1¼oz/2½ tbsp butter
1 onion, finely chopped
675g/1½lb Savoy cabbage, finely
  shredded
5ml/1 tsp caraway seeds
1.5 litres/2½ pints/6¼ cups chicken stock
30ml/2 tbsp plain (all-purpose) flour
15ml/1 tbsp creamed horseradish
30ml/2 tbsp crème fraîche
115g/4oz/1¼ cups freshly grated
  Parmesan cheese
salt and ground black pepper

Cream of Cabbage and Horseradish Soup
Tormás káposztakrémleves

This is a perfect combination: smooth and creamy Savoy cabbage with a hint of horseradish. Hungarians use freshly grated horseradish root, but this recipe is a little milder and uses creamed horseradish instead.

1 Melt 10g/¼oz/½ tbsp butter in a large pan and add the onion. Fry gently for 1 minute, then add the cabbage. Stir well and add the caraway seeds. Pour in the chicken stock and then cook for around 10–15 minutes.

2 Meanwhile, make a roux by heating the remaining butter in a small frying pan and adding the flour. Stir the roux and then cook until smooth, gradually adding some of the hot stock from the soup to combine with the roux.

3 Return the roux mixture to the pan with the soup. Stir well to combine and season with salt and pepper. Add the horseradish and stir well. Cook for 15 minutes more.

4 Remove from the heat and blend the soup in a food processor or blender until smooth. Return to the pan and add the crème fraîche. Serve the soup hot, topped with Parmesan cheese.

PER SERVING: Energy 202kcal/841kJ; Protein 11g; Carbohydrate 11g, of which sugars 6g; Fat 13g, of which saturates 8g; Cholesterol 24mg; Calcium 278mg; Fibre 4g; Sodium 663mg

Serves 6

1.2kg/2½lb summer squash (courgettes (zucchini), marrow (large zucchini), yellow crookneck squash, yellow straightneck squash, and scallop squash), with skin, seeds removed and flesh cut into squares

60–90ml/4–6 tbsp olive oil

4 shallots, finely chopped

30ml/2 tbsp cognac

115g/4oz/1 cup of chestnuts, skinned and chopped

200ml/7fl oz/scant 1 cup sour cream

200ml/7fl oz/scant 1 cup vegetable stock

5ml/1 tsp finely chopped marjoram

5ml/1 tsp finely chopped fresh sage

115g/4oz/1 cup shelled pecan nuts, toasted and coarsely chopped

salt and ground black pepper

Squash Soup with Chestnuts
Gesztenyés sütőtökleves

Chestnuts and squash make natural partners. Chestnuts are used in Hungarian dishes throughout the year, either fresh or preserved. Use summer squash as they have tender flesh that needs a minimum of cooking.

1 Preheat the oven to 190°C/375°F/Gas 5. Put the squash in a roasting pan, coat with 45ml/3 tbsp olive oil, and bake in the oven for at least 1 hour. Cool and scoop out the soft flesh, together with any cooking juices, into a small container. Discard the skin.

2 In a medium pan, heat the remaining oil and fry the shallots over medium heat for 2–3 minutes, or until soft. Add the cognac and simmer over low heat until almost all the liquid has evaporated. Add the chestnuts and fry for 3 minutes.

3 Add the squash to the pan and remove from the heat, mixing well. Put the mixture in a food processor or blender and purée until soft, adding some sour cream and vegetable stock to help the blending.

4 Return the soup to the pan, and add more sour cream and stock to achieve the desired consistency. Season with salt and pepper. Cook over low heat for 10–15 minutes. Finally, add the herbs. Serve the soup hot, sprinkled with the pecan nuts and garnished with marjoram.

PER SERVING: Energy 392/1621kJ; Protein 5g; Carbohydrate 16g, of which sugars 9g; Fat 34g, of which saturates 7g; Cholesterol 20mg; Calcium 98mg; Fibre 3.7g; Sodium 182mg

Serves 6

300g/11oz field (portabello) mushrooms
30ml/2 tbsp olive oil
2 shallots, finely chopped
600ml/1 pint/2½ cups vegetable stock
30ml/2 tbsp fresh tarragon, chopped
45ml/3 tbsp sour cream
salt and ground black pepper
slices of wholegrain bread, to serve

COOK'S TIP

When sautéing the mushrooms use a
large pan to maximize the cooking heat.

Mushroom and Tarragon Soup
Tárkonyos gombaleves

This delightful combination of ingredients sees the
earthy flavours of the mushrooms combine with the sour
cream and fresh tarragon to produce a satisfying and
warming appetizer or main meal.

1 Clean and slice the mushrooms
quite finely.

2 Add the olive oil to a large pan and
heat gently. Add shallots, sauté for
2–3 minutes and add the
mushrooms. Sauté for 5 minutes.

3 Add the stock and season. Simmer
for 15–20 minutes, covered.

4 When the soup has thickened, add
the tarragon and remove the soup
from the heat.

5 Add the sour cream and mix to
combine, while the soup is still hot.
Serve, garnished with tarragon, and
accompanied with crusty bread.

PER SERVING: Energy 329kcal/1356kJ; Protein 1g; Carbohydrate 5g, of which sugars 15g; Fat 35g, of which saturates 6g; Cholesterol 5mg; Calcium 15mg; Fibre 1.3g; Sodium 268mg

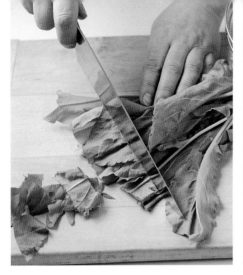  

Sorrel Soup with Spaetzle

Sóskaleves galuskával

Sorrel is a green that heralds the onset of spring. It is easy to grow and should be picked when the leaves are still tender. It can also be prepared with spinach or watercress. Hungarian dumplings can be served with the soup if you prefer, instead of the spaetzle.

Serves 6
5ml/1 tsp olive oil
250g/9oz fresh sorrel leaves, roughly
    chopped
10g/¼oz/½ tbsp butter
30ml/2 tbsp cornflour (cornstarch)
1 litre/1¾ pints/4 cups light chicken
    stock
1.5ml/¼ tsp grated nutmeg
45ml/3 tbsp crème fraîche
salt and ground black pepper
dill sprigs, to garnish

For the spaetzle
65g/2½oz/9 tbsp plain
    (all-purpose) flour
1 egg
1 egg yolk
5ml/1 tsp crème fraîche
60ml/4 tbsp warm milk

COOK'S TIP
You can serve this dish with Hungarian Dumplings (see pages 64–65).

VARIATION
This soup also works well with wild nettles – in which case, simply replace the sorrel leaves with the equivalent weight of nettles.

1 Put the olive oil in a large pan and fry the sorrel leaves gently, stirring, until wilted.

2 Melt the butter in another large pan over medium heat. Add the cornflour and stir to make a smooth roux. Gradually add the chicken stock, stirring to combine, and then add the wilted sorrel leaves.

3 Season to taste and add the nutmeg. Bring to a gentle boil and then reduce to a simmer for 15 minutes. Add the crème fraîche and remove from the heat.

4 To make the spaetzle, combine the flour, egg, egg yolk and crème fraîche in a bowl, and mix well. Season with salt and pepper. Gradually add the warm milk and keep working the mixture until it forms a smooth, thick dough. Add more liquid or flour to get the right consistency.

5 With the dough on a cutting board hold the board above a pan of boiling water and scrape off a small amount of dough into the hot soup. Spaetzle need to be small, so each dough scraping should be about the length of a teaspoon bowl.

6 Return the soup to a simmer and cook for a further 10 minutes, or until the spaetzle are cooked through, indicated by the point at which the dumplings rise to the top of the soup. Serve sprinkled with fresh dill.

COOK'S TIP
Spaetzle presses can be used for making the spaetzle shapes, and are relatively inexpensive. One of the most popular has a flat body with perforated holes. This is positioned over a pot of boiling water, filled with dough and moved back and forth so that the dough drops into the water. Another example has a hinge that compresses the dough. You could also use a potato ricer.

PER SERVING: Energy 151kcal/629kJ; Protein 5g; Carbohydrate 14g, of which sugars 1g; Fat 9g, of which saturates 4g; Cholesterol 86mg; Calcium 140mg; Fibre 2.1g; Sodium 578mg

Serves 6

50g/2oz pancetta or streaky (fatty) smoked bacon, cut into cubes

1 onion, finely chopped

150g/5oz/generous ⅔ cup dried yellow peas

115g/4oz/½ cup red lentils

5ml/1 tsp sweet paprika

2.5ml/½ tsp ground cumin

1.5 litres/2½ pints/6¼ cups chicken stock

8 parsley sprigs, leaves finely chopped

salt and ground black pepper

rye bread, to serve

Yellow Pea and Red Lentil Soup

Sárgaborsóleves vöröslencsével

Perfect for soups, vegetable purées and stews, pulses feature heavily in Hungarian cuisine and there is a vast variety to be found at the markets. Yellow peas are rich and buttery and red lentils have a sweet, nutty flavour – together they provide a high-protein dish.

1 Put the bacon in a large pan over medium-high heat. Stir and cook for 2–3 minutes, or until golden. Add the onion and continue cooking over low heat for 3 minutes.

2 Add the yellow peas and red lentils, and stir to coat well. Season to taste, add the paprika and cumin, and then the stock.

3 Simmer over medium heat for 1 hour. Sprinkle with the parsley and serve with some rye bread.

COOK'S TIPS

• Lentils have a high protein content, so combined with the pancetta or bacon they increase the protein content of the meal.

• Lentils that have been in the storecupboard are fine to use but will need a longer cooking time, so avoid mixing newly bought lentils with old ones.

PER SERVING: Energy 179kcal/757kJ; Protein 12g; Carbohydrate 28g, of which sugars 2g; Fat 3g, of which saturates 1g; Cholesterol 5mg; Calcium 31mg; Fibre 5.1g; Sodium 581mg

Serves 6

250g/9oz smoked pork shank, boned and
soaked overnight

1 onion, halved

2 bay leaves

2 carrots, chopped into small cubes

2 celery sticks, with leaves, chopped into
small cubes

1/2 swede (rutabaga), chopped into small
cubes

200g/7oz smoked sausage, chopped
roughly

400g/14oz can red kidney beans, drained
and rinsed

15g/1/2oz /1 tbsp butter

30ml/2 tbsp cornflour (cornstarch)

5ml/1 tsp sweet paprika

5ml/1 tsp olive oil

4 garlic cloves, finely sliced

salt and ground black pepper

Ham Shank Soup

Jókai bableves

This soup is also known as Jokai soup, named after the
famous Hungarian novelist, Mor Jokai, who adored this
dish. It is a hearty, substantial and one-pot soup,
containing red kidney beans, vegetables and smoked
sausage as well as a smoked pork shank. For even more
Hungarian authenticity, top the soup with your favourite
dumplings just before serving.

1 Put the pork shank in a large pan
with the onion and bay leaves. Cover
with water and bring to a simmer over
low heat. Cook for 1 hour.

2 Add the carrots, celery and swede to
the pan and season to taste. Add the
sausage, cover the pan and cook for
20 minutes.

3 Remove the pork from the large pan
and chop into fairly small chunks,
then return to the pan along with the
kidney beans.

4 Meanwhile, melt the butter in a small
pan and add the cornflour, stirring to
make a roux. Stir in about 250ml/
8fl oz/1 cup of the soup, to make a
thick purée, then add to the pan with
the pork and vegetables and stir in to
thicken. Add the paprika and stir.

5 Heat the olive oil in a small pan and
add the garlic. Sauté for 1 minute,
until just golden, then remove with a
slotted spoon and drain on kitchen
paper. Serve the soup topped with the
sautéed garlic slices.

PER SERVING: Energy 273kcal/1141kJ; Protein 19g; Carbohydrate 21g, of which sugars 9g; Fat 13g, of which saturates 5g; Cholesterol 32mg; Calcium 83mg; Fibre 6.3g; Sodium 496mg

Chicken Soup
Újházi tyúkhúsleves

This chicken soup is named after an actor called Ede Ujhazi (1844–1915) who, after being disappointed with some chicken soup that he tasted in a small Budapest restaurant, remodelled the recipe, which was then adopted throughout the region. It is associated with the famous Gundel restaurant, still among the most prestigious in Budapest. Traditionally, this soup would have used older and therefore tougher hens that would have needed a longer cooking time, but young chickens are used more commonly now. The soup is often served with home-made dumplings.

Serves 6

1 chicken, about 1.2kg/2½lb, cut into
  8 pieces
3 carrots, chopped
2 celery sticks, with leaves, chopped
1 large parsnip, chopped
1 kohlrabi, chopped
1 leek, chopped
5 green peppercorns
1 bay leaf
6–8 parsley sprigs
115g/4oz/1¾ cups sliced mushrooms
150g/5oz fine vermicelli pasta, broken
  into small pieces
6 flat leaf parsley sprigs, finely chopped
salt and ground black pepper

COOK'S TIP
When tasting the soup, use a stainless steel spoon – spoons made of wood or silver will disguise the flavour.

1 Put the chicken pieces into a large pan and cover with cold water. Add the carrots, celery, parsnip, kohlrabi and leek to the pan.

2 Season to taste with salt and pepper, add the green peppercorns, bay leaf and parsley, and bring to a simmer over low heat. Cover and cook for 1 hour, skimming occasionally.

3 Put a large sieve (strainer) over another pan and pour the soup through. Remove the chicken and discard the celery, peppercorns, bay leaf and parsley. Remove and discard the chicken skin.

4 Finely chop the remaining vegetables from the pan and add to the soup stock, then remove the chicken meat from the bones and add to the soup. Discard the bones.

5 Add the mushrooms and vermicelli and cook for 5 minutes more. Sprinkle with parsley and serve hot.

PER SERVING: Energy 290kcal/1217kJ; Protein 26g; Carbohydrate 31g, of which sugars 8g; Fat 7g, of which saturates 2g; Cholesterol 88mg; Calcium 87mg; Fibre 5.2g; Sodium 155mg

Hungarian Goulash
Gulyásleves

Here is the traditional recipe for this hearty dish, named after the herdsmen (*gulyás*) who prepared the meal in a cast-iron kettle over an open fire as they were working in the pasture. In the West we tend to eat goulash as a stew, but Hungarian goulash is a thin soup with plenty of meat and vegetables. Whether you describe it as a chunky stew or a warming main dish, it can be prepared in advance and is therefore ideal to use for a party or family gathering. Two ingredients are of utmost importance: paprika and caraway. These spices are what gives goulash its unique flavour.

Serves 6
45ml/3 tbsp vegetable oil
1 large onion, chopped
800g/1³/₄lb good-quality stewing beef,
 cut into 2.5cm/1in cubes
1 garlic clove, crushed
2.5ml/¹/₂ tsp caraway seeds
30ml/2 tbsp sweet paprika
2 tomatoes, chopped
1 green (bell) pepper, seeded and
 thinly sliced
300g/11oz potatoes, peeled and cubed
salt and ground black pepper
Hungarian dumplings, to serve (see
 pages 64–65)

1 Heat the oil in a heavy pan or flameproof casserole dish over medium heat and gently fry the onion until soft without browning. When the onion turns transparent, add the beef and stir to sauté the meat with the onions. Add the garlic and caraway seeds.

2 Take the pan or casserole off the heat and add the paprika (see Cook's Tip), stirring constantly to make sure that the paprika is absorbed well by the meat. Add 1.5 litres/2¹/₂ pints/6¹/₄ cups water and simmer gently for at least 1 hour.

3 Check that the meat is cooked by testing a small piece. If you are happy with it, add the tomatoes, green pepper and potatoes. Otherwise, cook for about 20 minutes longer before you add the vegetables. Season to taste and simmer for a further 30 minutes.

4 For an authentic combination, serve hot accompanied by galuska, the dumplings that are traditionally served with goulash.

VARIATIONS
Because gulyás is so popular there are a number of variations: babgulyás has white beans added to the ingredients (canned or pre-cooked), székelygulás has sauerkraut added, and polócgulyás green beans.

COOK'S TIP
Paprika is never added over direct heat.The pan must be removed from the heat to add the paprika, because paprika has a high sugar content; if added directly over the heat it would burn and become bitter in taste.

PER SERVING: Energy 320kcal/1336kJ; Protein 31g; Carbohydrate 14g, of which sugars 4g; Fat 16g, of which saturates 4g; Cholesterol 84mg; Calcium 29mg; Fibre 2.3g; Sodium 160mg

Serves 6

1 cauliflower, trimmed and cut into
 florets
1.5 litres/2½ pints/6¼ cups chicken stock
20g/¾oz/1½ tbsp butter
30ml/2 tbsp plain (all-purpose) flour
150ml/¼ pint/⅔ cup sour cream
115g/4oz/1½ cups fresh porcini
 mushrooms, cleaned, thinly sliced
2 tarragon sprigs, leaves finely chopped
salt and ground black pepper

Cauliflower and Porcini Soup
Vargányás karfiolleves

Sour cream and mushroom are classic soup ingredients and this version uses cauliflower
topped with fine slices of porcini, also known as ceps. Hungarians are very fond of picking
wild mushrooms, and porcini are among the most common ones found during the
mushroom season. Any variety of wild mushroom will taste good in this soup.

1 Put the cauliflower in a large pan
with the chicken stock and bring to
the boil. Season to taste with salt and
pepper. Reduce to a simmer and
cook for 10 minutes, or until the
cauliflower is tender.

2 Put 15g/½oz/1 tbsp butter into a
small pan and melt over gentle heat.
Add the flour and stir to combine to
make a smooth roux. Add some of the
cooking liquid from the cauliflower to
the roux and combine, then gradually
add to the pan with the cauliflower
and the sour cream, stirring well.

3 Simmer for 10 minutes and adjust
the seasoning. Remove from the heat
and process in a food processor until
smooth. Return to the pan.

4 Melt the remaining butter in a frying
pan and, when just foaming, add the
sliced porcini and cook until golden on
each side. Remove and drain on
kitchen paper. Divide the soup among
bowls, arrange a few porcini slices on
top, and sprinkle with the tarragon.

PER SERVING: Energy 123kcal/512kJ; Protein 5g; Carbohydrate 6g, of which sugars 3g; Fat 9g, of which saturates 5g; Cholesterol 22mg; Calcium 49mg; Fibre 2.1g; Sodium 441mg

Serves 6

10g/¼oz/½ tbsp butter
1 onion, chopped
200g/7oz smoked bacon, cut into
   chunky dice
30ml/2 tbsp barley
500g/1¼lb sauerkraut, chopped
7.5ml/1½ tsp sweet paprika
3–4 sage sprigs, leaves finely sliced
60ml/4 tbsp sour cream
salt and ground black pepper

Sauerkraut and Smoked Bacon Soup
Savanyúkáposzta-leves angolszalonnával

Pickled cabbage, sauerkraut, is very common all over eastern and central Europe.
It appears in many recipes from Hungary, where it is well known for its restorative powers
as well as being enjoyed for its taste alone. Although sauerkraut is sold in most food
shops, it is at its best when home-made.

1 Melt the butter in a large pan over medium heat and add the onion and bacon. Cook gently for 2–3 minutes,

2 Add the barley and sauerkraut and mix to combine with the onions and bacon. Then cook for 5 minutes, stirring well.

3 Sprinkle with the paprika and add 1.5 litres/2½ pints/6¼ cups water, then bring to the boil.

4 Simmer over medium heat for 20–30 minutes, stirring occasionally. Adjust the seasoning. Serve the thick soup with sage leaves on top and a spoonful of the sour cream.

COOK'S TIP
To make your own sauerkraut, see the instructions on page 17.

VARIATIONS
• To create a meatier soup, add smoked hocks or a ham bone.
• You can use roux or potatoes to thicken the soup instead of barley.

PER SERVING: Energy 155kcal/643kJ; Protein 9g; Carbohydrate 8g, of which sugars 3g; Fat 10g, of which saturates 5g; Cholesterol 33mg; Calcium 62mg; Fibre 0.7g; Sodium 1086mg

APPETIZERS

Most sizeable Hungarian meals, typically lunchtime ones, begin with soup. However, appetizers can offer a delicious alternative. These are often served on a summer's day, with the sun blazing down, and all that is needed to start the meal is a platter of carefully arranged chilled salad vegetables and sliced ham or delicate cottage cheese. Many of these recipes can also work well as canapés at a party, as a snack, or even as a light meal in themselves, accompanied by a loaf of good bread and a glass of wine or fruit juice.

Light delights and herby flavours

The recipes in this chapter are full of traditional Hungarian ingredients. Many are based on the light dairy products that were made locally in country areas. These include cottage cheese from cow's milk and feta cheese from sheep's milk, both of which have a light tangy taste and are low in fat. They absorb the flavours of herbs and spices to perfection – paprika, in particular, but also horseradish, caraway seeds and garden herbs. Some of these recipes are simple blends of cheese, sour cream and spices, used as a dip or a topping for bread, while others are more elaborate mixtures bound with breadcrumbs and fried for a crunchy treat. Most of these are equally delicious served hot or cold.

Despite the scarcity of saltwater fish and shellfish in this landlocked country, plenty of fish crop up in appetizers and main courses. Salmon, pike and carp are to be found in the many beautiful rivers and lakes. Salmon fillets make a tasty variation on croquettes, where the mixture is formed into tiny sausage shapes wrapped around a dot of garlic butter and fried in breadcrumbs. You can make a small amount of fish such as a pike fillet go a long way by blending it with chopped apples, sour cream and butter into a dip or pâté, and serving it on thinly sliced toast – a perfect light summer supper.

Large, flat field (portabello) mushrooms make a good base for an appetizer – a simple mixture of soft cheese, herbs and crisply fried diced bacon sits on top of the mushrooms and they are then baked in the oven until the cheese melts and the bacon browns.

Grains such as pearl barley are not just used for soups. An appetizer or summer dish is based on this light, tender cooked grain, blended with ingredients such as salad vegetables, fruit and nuts to make a tasty chilled mixture coated in a citrus dressing. This shows the Hungarian delight in mixing sweet and savoury flavours.

The last recipe here, White Bean and Goat's Cheese Salad with Sour Cream Pesto, is a cornucopia of flavours. It has cold sliced meats, hard-boiled eggs, vegetables and salad ingredients, including the spicy pickled gherkins and strong mustard beloved of Hungarians. The mayonnaise is lightened with the addition of chopped hardboiled egg – a technique that is found in other nearby European countries.

Feta and Paprika Bruschetta
Feta sajtos melegszendvics

These are among the most common snacks in Hungary and central Europe. My mother used to make a large quantity and keep them in the refrigerator for quick and healthy bites to eat. It is very common to add butter to the cheese mixture, but here it is lightened by adding some cream cheese instead.

Serves 6

300g/11oz/3 cups creamy sheep's feta cheese, crumbed
150g/5oz/generous ²/₃ cup cream cheese
2.5ml/¹/₂ tsp mustard powder
5ml/1 tsp ground cumin
2.5ml/¹/₂ tsp sweet paprika
15ml/1 tbsp cognac
salt and ground black pepper
tomato salad, to serve

For the bruschetta

12 thin slices of ciabatta bread
30ml/2 tbsp olive oil
2.5ml/¹/₂ tsp sweet paprika
1 small red onion, sliced thinly

1 Put the feta and cream cheeses in a bowl and mix to combine until achieving a creamy texture. Season to taste, remembering that feta cheese is already rather salty.

2 Add the dry mustard powder, cumin and paprika. Stir to combine, then add the cognac and stir again.

3 Preheat the grill (broiler) to medium. Arrange the ciabatta bread slices on a tray and put under the grill for 1–2 minutes on each side, until they turn a golden colour.

4 Remove the slices and drizzle lightly with the olive oil, and then add a sprinkle of paprika.

5 Spoon some of the feta and paprika mixture over the bread and arrange the red onion slices over the top. Serve with a fresh tomato salad.

VARIATIONS
• Replace the bruschetta with grilled sour dough bread, slices of baguette or your favourite crackers.
• Use any cheese of your choice, or a combination of white and soft cheeses, but a lovely, creamy feta cheese is always a hit.

SERVING SUGGESTIONS
Serve the bruschetta with a salad, with pasta or with hot or cold meats.

PER SERVING: Energy 247/1027kJ; Protein 10g; Carbohydrate 12g, of which sugars 2g; Fat 17g, of which saturates 8g; Cholesterol 37mg; Calcium 213mg; Fibre 0.2g; Sodium 901mg

Serves 4

300g/11oz/4½ cups mushrooms
oil, for greasing
185g/6½oz smoked bacon, cut into
  small cubes
250g/9oz/generous 1 cup ricotta
  cheese
8 thyme sprigs, leaves finely
  chopped
salt and ground black pepper
green mixed leaf salad, to serve

Transylvanian Stuffed Mushrooms
Erdélyi töltött gombafejek

This dish is usually served with creamy polenta or cornmeal, the staple ingredients of the Transylvanian shepherds' diet. Because of this frequent pairing of ingredients, this dish is also known as 'shepherd's mushrooms'. Ricotta cheese is used here, but home-made cottage cheese would have been a traditional choice.

1 Preheat the oven to 180°C/350°F/ Gas 4. Remove the stems from the mushrooms and reserve for another dish. Arrange the mushrooms on a greased baking tray.

2 Cook the bacon in a non-stick pan over medium-high heat until golden brown. Remove the bacon and put in a bowl to cool. Season with salt and pepper.

3 Add the ricotta cheese and thyme. Mix well to combine. Spoon into the prepared mushrooms, piling in the filling.

4 Cook the stuffed mushrooms in the oven for 10–12 minutes, or until the tops are melting and golden. Remove and serve with a crisp green salad.

COOK'S TIP
Clean the mushrooms before preparation by wiping each one with a damp cloth.

PER SERVING: Energy 244kcal/1012kJ; Protein 16g; Carbohydrate 2g, of which sugars 1g; Fat 19g, of which saturates 8g; Cholesterol 61mg; Calcium 160mg; Fibre 1.7g; Sodium 825

Serves 4

300g/11oz/scant 1½ cups túró curd
(farmer's) cheese or cottage cheese
115g/4oz/½ cup cream cheese
1 small bunch of spring onions
(scallions), finely chopped
30ml/2 tbsp sour cream
15ml/1 tbsp sweet paprika
30ml/2 tbsp caraway seeds
2.5ml/½ tsp mustard powder
1 garlic clove, crushed
small bunch of chives, finely chopped
salt and ground black pepper
toasted crusty bread, to serve

Cottage Cheese and Sweet Paprika Dip
Körözött

Paprika is the star ingredient of this spicy dip and makes a frequent appearance in other dips from the region. Sweet paprika is often used in combination with yogurt, cream cheese or mayonnaise as well as avocado or artichoke, but here we have a low-fat variation with cottage cheese. Use to accompany pre-supper drinks, as an appetizer or a side dish.

1 Put the túró curd cheese or cottage cheese and cream cheese into a bowl and season to taste with a little salt and ground black pepper.

2 Add the chopped spring onions, sour cream, paprika, caraway seeds, mustard powder, garlic and fresh chives. Stir together well, then serve with toasted crusty bread.

VARIATION
You can prepare this recipe only with cream cheese if you want a smoother texture and are not worried about the extra calories.

SERVING IDEAS
This ideal party dip can be served with chicken pieces and crudités such as pieces of chicken, green beans, cherry tomatoes and carrot sticks.

PER SERVING: Energy 237kcal/984kJ; Protein 12g; Carbohydrate 6g, of which sugars 5g; Fat 19g, of which saturates 11g; Cholesterol 44mg; Calcium 193mg; Fibre 0.8g; Sodium 418mg

Serves 4–6

250g/9oz/1¼ cups pearl barley
2 large ripe tomatoes, finely diced
½ green (bell) pepper, seeded and
chopped
½ cucumber, peeled and
finely sliced
75g/3oz/¾ cup white seedless
grapes, halved
1 small garlic clove, crushed
60ml/4 tbsp olive oil
juice of 1½ lemons, plus 45ml/3 tbsp
75ml/5 tbsp chopped fresh parsley
45ml/3 tbsp chopped fresh mint
45ml/3 tbsp shelled pistachio nuts,
lightly toasted
30ml/2 tbsp olive oil
salt and ground black pepper

VARIATION

For extra visual texture use half the
amount of pearl barley and the other
half of black barley.

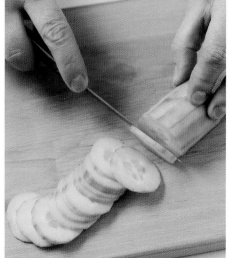

Pearl Barley Salad with Grapes and Pistachio Nuts
Szőlős-pisztáciás árpagyöngy saláta

Hungarians love grains, and this salad is a modern version of a quick city lunch. For a more substantial meal, it can be topped with cheese or grilled sausage.

1 Cook the barley in plenty of boiling water for 15–20 minutes, or until soft. Drain well and keep to one side.

2 In a large bowl mix together the tomatoes, green pepper, cucumber, grapes and garlic. Add the barley and mix well. Season with salt and pepper, then add 40ml/2½ tbsp olive oil and the juice of 1½ lemons, and mix in the parsley and mint.

3 Leave the salad to stand in the refrigerator for about 2 hours. Just before serving, scatter the pistachio nuts over and drizzle with the remaining olive oil and lemon juice.

COOK'S TIPS

• Pearl barley is a wonderfully healthy ingredient – it is high in fibre, cholesterol-free and virtually free of fat.
• You can also prepare pearl barley using a rice cooker. Simply add 2½ cups water per cup of barley.

PER SERVING: Energy 334kcal/1401kJ; Protein 5g; Carbohydrate 39g, of which sugars 4g; Fat 19g, of which saturates 3g; Cholesterol 0mg; Calcium 29mg; Fibre 3.5g; Sodium 98mg

Serves 6

200g/7oz piece cooked ham, diced
3 frankfurters, sliced
1 large potato, boiled, peeled and diced
1 large carrot, boiled and diced
115g/4oz/1 cup cooked peas
2 gherkins, diced
2 eggs, hard-boiled, shelled and diced
50g/2oz freshly cooked green beans,
　chopped
7.5ml/1½ tsp Dijon mustard
30ml/2 tbsp chopped fresh parsley
salt and ground black pepper

For the mayonnaise

1 egg
1 hard-boiled egg yolk
150ml/¼ pint/⅔ cup olive oil
30ml/2 tbsp lemon juice

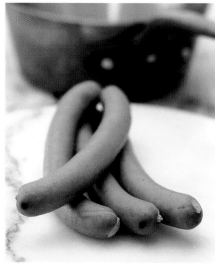

Hungarian Cold Buffet Salad with Mustard

Magyaros mustáros hidegsaláta

Buffets are much loved by Hungarians, and this salad is a must on every cold buffet table. It is, in fact, good enough for a main course, because it has everything in it: meat, eggs and cooked vegetables. If you can, use Hungarian sausages and salami.

1 For the mayonnaise, put the raw egg and the cooked egg yolk into a food processor or blender and season. Blend well.

2 With the motor running, add a fine stream of olive oil slowly – if you add it too quickly the consistency will be more like a sauce than a creamy mayonnaise. Add the lemon juice and store in the refrigerator until needed.

3 In a large bowl, mix the ham, frankfurters, potato, carrot, peas, gherkins, eggs, beans and mustard, then season to taste. Add about 60ml/4 tbsp mayonnaise and mix together, making sure that you don't crush the vegetables. Add the parsley before you serve the salad, with the rest of the mayonnaise.

PER SERVING: Energy 455kcal/1883kJ; Protein 17g; Carbohydrate 10g, of which sugars 2g; Fat 39g, of which saturates 8g; Cholesterol 151mg; Calcium 41mg; Fibre 2.4g; Sodium 948mg

Serves 4

3 egg whites
350g/12oz feta cheese, finely crumbled
8 oregano sprigs, leaves finely chopped
60ml/4 tbsp fresh breadcrumbs
15ml/1 tbsp lightly toasted hazelnuts,
  finely chopped
45ml/3 tbsp olive oil
10g/¼oz/½ tbsp butter
salt and ground black pepper

For the salad

leaves from a small bunch of parsley
leaves from a small bunch of basil
leaves from a small bunch of chives
leaves from ½ bunch of mint
15ml/1 tbsp olive oil
juice of 1 small lemon
30ml/2 tbsp toasted hazelnuts, roughly
  chopped

Herb and Cheese Fritters
Fűszeres sült sajtgolyók

A quick and easy snack or a perfect appetizer. You can use any type of sheep's cheese, although feta cheese is best. These hot fritters should be served with a salad herb melange of parsley, basil, chives and mint.

1 Put the egg whites into a clean, grease-free bowl and whisk until they form stiff peaks. Add the grated cheese and fold in carefully to combine with the egg whites. Season to taste with salt and pepper. Add the oregano and mix to combine.

2 Shape the mixture into small balls. Put the breadcrumbs and chopped hazelnuts in a bowl and mix to combine. Roll each of the cheese balls into the mixture and put them on a tray.

3 Heat the oil and butter in a non-stick pan and, when hot, add the cheese balls and sauté on all sides for 2–3 minutes, or until golden brown.

4 To make the salad, mix all the herbs in a large bowl, drizzle with olive oil and lemon juice, then season to taste. Add the toasted hazelnuts on top. Serve the cheese fritters hot with the fresh herb salad.

PER SERVING: Energy 443kcal/1834kJ; Protein 18g; Carbohydrate 8g, of which sugars 2g; Fat 38g, of which saturates 16g; Cholesterol 67mg; Calcium 345mg; Fibre 1.0g; Sodium 1379mg

Serves 6

200g/7oz fresh pike fillets, bones
   removed
50g/2oz/¼ cup butter, softened
15ml/1 tbsp creamed horseradish
   (or horseradish sauce below)
5ml/1 tsp sour cream
a pinch of caster (superfine) sugar
2 small eating apples
ground black pepper

For the horseradish sauce

45ml/3 tbsp grated fresh horseradish
15ml/1 tbsp white wine vinegar
10ml/2 tsp caster (superfine) sugar
150ml/¼ pint/⅔ cup double (heavy) cream

To serve

6 slices rye bread
1 small red onion, sliced into rings
1 large apple, cored and sliced into rings,
   tossed in the juice of 1 lemon
50ml/2fl oz/¼ cup sour cream
6 parsley sprigs

Pike and Horseradish Pâté
Tormás csukapástétom

With no sea coast, Hungarian fish dishes are not commonplace. So recipes from the region using fish will feature freshwater varieties such as catfish, carp, pike and perch. Pike has lean, firm, bony flesh and a delicate flavour, and forms a classic taste experience when combined with horseradish and sour cream.

1 To make the horseradish sauce, put the horseradish, vinegar and sugar into a bowl and mix well. Whip the cream until it is thickened and fold in the horseradish mixture. Cover and chill the sauce.

2 Chop the pike fillets into pieces and put in a food processor or blender with the butter, creamed horseradish, sour cream, sugar and black pepper to taste.

3 Pulse the fish and the horseradish sauce until it is smooth but not minced (ground).

4 Peel the apples and grate finely, adding them to the fish mixture. Mix well and chill until ready to use.

5 To serve, spread the pâté on to the rye bread, and top with the onion and apple rings. Finish with a small dollop of sour cream and a sprig of parsley.

COOK'S TIPS

• If you are unable to find any fresh horseradish root, use preserved grated horseradish instead.
• For a lighter sauce, replace half the cream with thick natural (plain) yogurt.

PER SERVING: Energy 220kcal/921kJ; Protein 9g; Carbohydrate 23g, of which sugars 11g; Fat 11g, of which saturates 6g; Cholesterol 40mg; Calcium 48mg; Fibre 2.9g; Sodium 324mg

Salmon Croquettes
Lazackrokett

Croquettes are small savoury or sweet preparations, and are very typically offered as a canapé or appetizer in Hungarian cuisine. Mostly they are made from potatoes, but croquettes can also be made with veal, chicken, mushrooms, rice or fish.

Makes 20–25
500g/1¼lb salmon fillet, skin and bones removed
2 slices white bread
100ml/3½fl oz/scant ½ cup milk
1 large egg, beaten
30ml/2 tbsp finely chopped fresh dill
150g/5oz/10 tbsp butter
2–3 garlic cloves, crushed
200g/7oz/3½ cups brioche breadcrumbs, toasted
vegetable oil, for shallow-frying
salt and ground black pepper

For the horseradish mayonnaise
200g/7oz/scant 1 cup good-quality mayonnaise
30ml/2 tbsp sour cream
5ml/1 tsp French mustard
30ml/2 tbsp creamed horseradish
2.5ml/½ tsp fennel seeds, finely ground
about 15ml/1 tbsp fresh horseradish root, grated (optional)
about 30ml/2 tbsp lemon juice

1 To make the horseradish mayonnaise, put all the ingredients, except the horseradish root and lemon juice, in a large bowl and mix well. Adjust the flavours by adding the grated horseradish, if you like it hotter, and lemon juice to taste.

2 To make the croquettes, chop the fish finely. Soak the bread slices in the milk and squeeze out as much of the surplus liquid as possible.

3 Chop the bread into small pieces. Put the salmon, bread, egg, dill, and salt and pepper to taste, in a food processor or blender, and process until smooth. Using your fingers, shape the salmon mixture into walnut-sized shapes and chill them.

4 Meanwhile, mix the butter and garlic together and shape into small hazelnut-sized shapes. Chill with the fish mixture for about 1 hour.

5 Remove the fish and garlic butter from the refrigerator. Insert a garlic-butter ball into the centre of each salmon ball, making sure that you seal the hole well.

6 Roll the salmon croquettes in the toasted brioche crumbs and chill until ready to use, for up to 2 hours.

7 Heat the oil in a large non-stick pan and cook the croquettes, a few at a time, turning so that all sides are evenly coloured, about 3–4 minutes per side. Serve hot, with the horseradish mayonnaise.

PER SERVING: Energy 203kcal/845kJ; Protein 6g; Carbohydrate 8g, of which sugars 1g; Fat 16g, of which saturates 5g; Cholesterol 44mg; Calcium 30mg; Fibre 0.6g; Sodium 183mg

White Bean and Goat's Cheese Salad with Sour Cream Pesto

Kecskesajtos fehérbabsaláta tejfölös pestóval

This delightfully easy recipe is an uplifting addition to the day as a side dish or a light lunch. The silky tang of the olive oil and the creamy beans combine beautifully with the flavours and textures of garlic, sour cream and pine nuts in the pesto.

Serves 4

10g/$\frac{1}{4}$oz/$\frac{1}{2}$ tbsp butter
1 shallot, chopped
1 carrot, chopped
500g/1$\frac{1}{4}$lb/3 cups dried cannellini or
    haricot (navy) beans, soaked overnight
    and drained
a handful each of fresh parsley, celery
    and thyme
juice of 2 lemons
60ml/4 tbsp extra virgin olive oil
2.5ml/$\frac{1}{2}$ tsp sweet paprika
200g/7oz goat's cheese, crumbled

For the sour cream pesto

130g/4$\frac{1}{2}$oz/generous 1 cup
    pine nuts
250ml/8fl oz/1 cup sour cream
2 garlic cloves, crushed
leaves from $\frac{1}{2}$ bunch parsley
leaves from $\frac{1}{2}$ bunch basil
juice of 1 lemon
40ml/2$\frac{1}{2}$ tbsp extra virgin olive oil
salt and ground black pepper

1 To make the sour cream pesto, put the pine nuts, sour cream, garlic and herbs into a food processor or blender. Process until well combined, then add the lemon juice and olive oil while the motor is still running. Season to taste. Adjust the seasoning.

2 Melt the butter in a large pan, add the shallot and carrot, and fry gently for 2 minutes. Add the beans, herbs and 350ml/12fl oz/1$\frac{1}{2}$ cups water, which should be enough to cover the beans.

3 Bring to the boil and then simmer for 30 minutes, or until the beans are tender. Drain and discard the herbs.

4 Add the lemon juice and olive oil, and season with salt, pepper and the paprika. Mix well and add the goat's cheese. Serve the bean salad with some sour cream pesto.

COOK'S TIP

Cannellini beans, also known as white kidney beans and fazolia beans, are a popular ingredient in Mediterranean countries, particularly Italy, and are enjoyed for their smooth consistency and nutty taste.

VARIATION

You can substitute cannellini beans with Great Northern or white haricot (navy) beans.

PER SERVING: Energy 896kcal/3715kJ; Protein 26g; Carbohydrate 30g, of which sugars 8g; Fat 76g, of which saturates 23g; Cholesterol 89mg; Calcium 249mg; Fibre 9.4g; Sodium 466mg

DUMPLINGS, PASTA AND PANCAKES

This chapter contains an array of recipes for the filling side dishes so beloved of Hungarians. Pasta is often made at home for the sheer pleasure of cooking something that is freshly made. Dumplings are quick to make and can be prepared in advance, cooked and frozen so that they are always available to add to a flavoursome soup or stew. Hungarian pancakes can be simple or elaborate, and are served in both savoury and sweet variations as an appetizer, main course or dessert, or an ideal party dish.

bites, morsels and pancake stacks

Hungarians love pasta, and most eat it as part of the meat course at least twice a week. It is also used as a quick dish for a light meal. The old tradition of avoiding meat on Fridays for religious reasons means that vegetarian or fish pasta dishes often feature on the Friday menu, at home and in restaurants. An unusual and typical feature of Hungarian cuisine is the sweet pasta recipes, such as poppy seed pasta in a honey and citrus dressing, topped with piquant goat's cheese. These work as a dessert or a main course.

As well as eating large pasta shapes such as wide, flat noodles, Hungarians enjoy tarhonya, which are little pasta pellets. These were introduced by the Ottoman Turks to Hungary in the 16th century. The process of making these is time-consuming, but they are still a feature in the diet, whether made at home or bought from the shops. The dough is pushed though a special strainer to form the correct shape and then spread out on large sheets to dry, ideally in the hot summer sun. Very often, flavourings such as paprika, onion or garlic are added to the pasta pellets. It is rare to find a cook who is willing to spend time making tarhonya at home these days, although some people still do so in the eastern region, on the part of the Great Hungarian Plain around the Tisza river.

Dumplings are a well-known feature of the Hungarian diet. These little balls of flour, eggs and butter or oil, mixed with herbs and other flavourings, are usually prepared to accompany soups and stews. Originally they would have been added to the stew to make the expensive ingredients, such as meat or fish, go a little further; today they are simply an essential part of the cuisine. Some dumplings can be prepared in advance and simmered in stock, then chilled or frozen before adding them to the finished meal. Others are better made fresh, and cooked just before the dish is served. The dumplings are always very small, a mere morsel of fluffy tastiness.

Pancakes are hugely popular, served simply with sugar, or piled high in a stack. The basic mixture is usually quite plain, and the variations are all in the filling, from strongly flavoured savoury mushrooms with sour cream to poppy seeds sweetened with sugar and vanilla.

Makes 20–22

300g/11oz brioche, cut into cubes
115g/4oz/1 cup plain (all-purpose) flour,
    plus extra for dusting
65g/2½oz/5 tbsp butter
a small bunch of fresh oregano, leaves
    finely chopped
5ml/1 tsp cumin seeds
250ml/8fl oz/1 cup milk
2 eggs, lightly beaten
200ml/7fl oz/scant 1 cup chicken stock
salt and ground black pepper

Oregano and Cumin Dumplings
Zsemlegombóc oregánóval

These lightly spiced dumplings are perfect to accompany any stew, soup or traditional
goulash. They can be cooked in large quantities and frozen to use when needed. This recipe
uses brioche, which gives the dumplings a light texture, but bread rolls can also be used.

1 Put the brioche and flour in a large bowl and add 5ml/1 tsp salt, stirring well to mix thoroughly.

2 Melt the butter in a wide-based pan and add the brioche mixture, the oregano and the cumin seeds, mixing well to combine.

3 Return the brioche mixture to the large bowl and add the milk and eggs. Stir with a wooden spoon to mix well, then leave to stand for 1 hour.

4 Using wet hands, form small rounds of the brioche mixture about 5cm (2in) in diameter, and put on a lightly floured tray.

5 Add the chicken stock to a pan of boiling water and cook the dumplings, a few at a time, until they rise to the surface.

6 Remove the dumplings and keep warm until you serve them, or cool and chill until needed. Serve with any soup, stew or goulash. Here they are served with Transylvanian Venison Stew (see pages 92–3).

PER SERVING: Energy 88kcal/370kJ; Protein 3g; Carbohydrate 11g, of which sugars 1g; Fat 4g, of which saturates 2g; Cholesterol 30mg; Calcium 50mg; Fibre 0.7g; Sodium 139mg

Serves 6
200g/7oz potatoes, peeled and grated
70g/2³/₄oz/7 tbsp potato flour
15ml/1 tbsp creamed horseradish
15ml/1 tbsp goose fat or butter
2 onions, finely sliced
30ml/2 tbsp pitted olives, chopped
15ml/1 tbsp chopped fresh parsley
salt and ground black pepper

Transylvanian Dumplings with Olives
Erdélyi galuska olívabogyóval

The origins of this recipe can be traced to Transylvania, where it is common to sauté dumplings in butter or goose fat (for a lighter option, simply substitute the goose fat with olive oil). In a new twist, this dish has been finished off with onions and olives.

1 Put the grated potatoes, potato flour and horseradish in a large bowl and mix together. Season with salt and pepper.

2 Using your fingers, tear off small walnut-sized pieces of the mixture, and drop them into a large pan of salted boiling water, a few at a time. Cook for 10 minutes, or until they rise to the surface. Remove with a slotted spoon and leave to drain in a colander.

3 Meanwhile, heat the goose fat or butter in a frying pan and fry the onions for 10 minutes over low heat, or until very soft. Add the olives.

4 Add the dumplings to the pan, and stir them gently so that they brown on all sides. Add the parsley and cook, stirring, for another 3–4 minutes. Serve them hot with any soup, stew or goulash.

PER SERVING: Energy 159kcal/671kJ; Protein 4g; Carbohydrate 28g, of which sugars 6g; Fat 4g, of which saturates 2g; Cholesterol 9mg; Calcium 30mg; Fibre 3.3g; Sodium 251mg

Hungarian Dumplings
Galuska (nokedli)

The most famous dumplings in Hungary, galuska are a traditional accompaniment to all porkölt dishes (the national paprika stew). Galuska are also commonly offered when serving goulash and soups. They can be made from different kinds of dough and are always small. One of the most memorable galuska taste experiences is served at the world-famous Gundel restaurant in Budapest.

Serves 6
2 eggs
about 300g/11oz/2⅔ cups plain
   (all-purpose) flour
45ml/3 tbsp finely chopped fresh mixed
   herbs, such as parsley, tarragon,
   thyme and rosemary
200g/7oz bacon, cubed finely
30ml/2 tbsp vegetable oil
salt
melted butter, to serve

1 Beat the eggs with 5ml/1 tsp salt and 200ml/7fl oz/scant 1 cup water. Add a little flour to make a smooth and thick mixture, then add the remaining flour and beat with a wooden spoon until the dough is glossy and exceptionally smooth.

2 Add the herbs and mix in well. Adjust the dough with more flour, if necessary, until it comes away from the sides of the bowl.

3 Place the dough on a board and, using a teaspoon, cut off noodles about 2.5cm/1in long and to the thickness of a pencil. Add the noodles to a pot of boiling water. Alternatively, push the dough through a dumpling strainer directly into the boiling water.

4 Cook until the galuska rise to the top of the water, then drain them in a colander.

5 Sauté the cubed bacon in a non-stick pan with the vegetable oil until golden and crispy. Serve the hot galuska as a light meal with some melted butter and topped with crispy bacon. Alternatively, serve with a soup or stew – here they are served with Chicken and Paprika Stew with Sour Cream (see pages 86–87).

PER SERVING: Energy 337kcal/1514kJ; Protein 13g; Carbohydrate 39g, of which sugars 1g; Fat 16g, of which saturates 5g; Cholesterol 102mg; Calcium 99mg; Fibre 2.4g; Sodium 626mg

Serves 6

60ml/4 tbsp butter, melted
2 eggs
6 dill sprigs, finely chopped
6 thyme sprigs, leaves finely chopped
6 parsley sprigs, leaves finely
  chopped
200g/7oz/generous 1 cup semolina
1 litre/1¾ pints/4 cups chicken stock

Herb Semolina Dumplings
Fűszeres daragaluska

These small semolina dumplings are perfect for soups, particularly a clear chicken broth. The herbs make them attractive as well as adding flavour. The light and fluffy little balls are delicate and tantalizingly tasty as they float on the soup.

1 Put the butter and eggs in a bowl and whisk until fluffy. Add the herbs and semolina and mix well.

2 Heat the chicken stock in a large pan to boiling point. Using a teaspoon, scoop off small amounts of the semolina mix to form the dumplings and drop them into the boiling stock.

3 Cook until the dumplings have risen to the top, and have become plump and fluffy.

4 Remove with a slotted spoon and add to a hot soup. Here the dumplings are served with Chicken Soup (see pages 36–37).

COOK'S TIPS
• Use coarse semolina, because finely ground semolina will create a denser dumpling that will cook more slowly.
• The dumplings can be made a few hours ahead of the meal – just cover them lightly with clear film (plastic wrap) so they don't dry out. Alternatively, they can be frozen until needed.

PER SERVING: Energy 227/953kJ; Protein 7g; Carbohydrate 26g, of which sugars 0g; Fat 11g, of which saturates 6g; Cholesterol 99mg; Calcium 24mg; Fibre 1.3g; Sodium 486mg

Serves 4
130g/4¹/₂oz/generous 1 cup plain
    (all-purpose) flour
1.5ml/¹/₄ tsp salt
1 egg
30ml/2 tbsp water
15ml/1 tbsp melted butter
fried bacon and sour cream (optional),
    to serve

Pinched Noodles
Csipetke

Something between a noodle and a dumpling, csipetke are served to accompany soups or stews. They are best cooked separately and then added to the dish, but they can also be served with bacon and sour cream as an accompaniment.

1 Put the flour, salt and egg in a bowl. Stir to combine and make a dough. Add a little water and knead until the dough is smooth and free from lumps. Wrap in clear film (plastic wrap) and chill for 30 minutes.

2 When ready to cook, remove from the refrigerator and allow to stand for 10 minutes. Roll to a 5mm/¹/₄in thickness and then pinch pieces off, roughly 2cm/³/₄in in size.

3 Have a large pan of boiling water ready and drop the dough pieces in, a few at a time. Cook until they are soft and have risen to the top, about 10–12 minutes.

4 Remove with a slotted spoon and toss in the melted butter. Either serve the dumplings on their own, accompanied by fried bacon and sour cream, or add to a soup or stew just before serving.

PER SERVING: Energy 161kcal/679kJ; Protein 5g; Carbohydrate 25g, of which sugars 1g; Fat 5g, of which saturates 2g; Cholesterol 66mg; Calcium 55mg; Fibre 1.2g; Sodium 168mg

Serves 4
300g/11oz dry wide egg noodles
6 rashers (strips) streaky (fatty) bacon,
    chopped
150g/5oz/generous 1½ cups cottage
    cheese
115g/4oz/½ cup mascarpone
200ml/7fl oz/scant 1 cup sour cream
5ml/1 tsp caraway seeds
salt and ground black pepper

Noodles with Cheese and Bacon Sauce
Túrós csusza

Noodle dishes are a regular favourite on the Hungarian table – loved either in their savoury or sweet form. Noodles can be served with almost anything, with cabbage, with potatoes, or with cottage cheese and bacon – and can even be served with honey for dessert.

1 Prepare the noodles according to the pack instructions and drain, then keep warm.

2 Cook the bacon in a non-stick pan over high heat until golden and crispy. Remove and add to the noodles. Stir to combine and season to taste.

3 Put the cottage cheese, mascarpone and sour cream in a pan and warm gently over low to medium heat. Season to taste with salt and pepper. Add this mixture to the noodles and toss lightly to combine.

4 Toast the caraway seeds lightly in a dry pan and sprinkle over the noodles to serve.

VARIATION
The recipe can be served as a dessert, in which case just replace the bacon with 30ml/2 tbsp soft light brown sugar or a drizzle of honey.

PER SERVING: Energy 655kcal/2378kJ; Protein 22g; Carbohydrate 58g, of which sugars 6g; Fat 39g, of which saturates 20g; Cholesterol 113mg; Calcium 145mg; Fibre 13.8g; Sodium 853mg

Serves 4
400g/14oz/3½ cups plain (all-purpose)
   flour
3 eggs
pinch of salt
115g/4oz/1 cup poppy seeds
grated rind of 1 orange
60ml/4 tbsp butter, melted
30ml/2 tbsp sugar
30ml/2 tbsp honey
150g/5oz goat's cheese, crumbled

Poppy Seed Pasta with Goat's Cheese
Mákos metélt kecskesajttal

This is best prepared using a pasta machine, so that you can make exceptionally thin layers.
If a machine is not available, roll out the pastry as thinly as you can. Here it is dressed with a
Hungarian favourite, poppy seeds, as well as butter, orange, honey and goat's cheese.

1 Sift the flour into a bowl and make
a well in the middle. Add the eggs
and salt. Mix roughly, then gradually
add 200–300ml/7fl oz–½ pint/scant
1–1¼ cups water. Keep mixing until
you have a soft and workable dough.

2 Knead for 10 minutes, then put the
dough in a bowl, cover with a dish
towel and allow to rest for 15 minutes.

3 Roll the dough as thinly as you can,
using either a pasta machine or a
rolling pin. This may take some time
– the dough needs to be paper-thin.
Cut into shapes of your choice,
perhaps long, thin strips or
rectangles or triangles. Traditionally,
this recipe would have used noodles.

4 Bring a large pan of water to the
boil and drop in the home-made
pasta. Cook for just 2–3 minutes, until
just tender. Drain and keep warm.

5 Add the poppy seeds, orange rind,
butter and sugar. Toss to combine.
Serve, drizzled with honey and topped
with goat's cheese.

PER SERVING: Energy 691kcal/2905kJ; Protein 29g; Carbohydrate 92g, of which sugars 16g; Fat 42g, of which saturates 18g; Cholesterol 241mg; Calcium 675mg; Fibre 3.6g; Sodium 489mg

Serves 8

15ml/1 tbsp butter, melted
500g/1¼lb/8 cups wild mushrooms,
  cleaned and roughly chopped
2 eggs
100ml/3½fl oz/scant ½ cup sour cream
115g/4oz/½ cup cream cheese
3–4 tarragon sprigs
8–10 pancakes (for method, see pancake
  recipe shown opposite)
melted butter, for brushing
115g/4oz/1 cup grated Cheddar cheese
salt and ground black pepper

Pancake and Wild Mushroom Stacks
Gombás rakott palacsinta

Stacks of filled pancakes are very common in Hungary and are often prepared for
a special dinner party, when they are served grandly as a table centrepiece. It is an
easy dish to prepare and you can pre-cook the pancakes well in advance, then assemble
them at the last minute with your desired filling. This stack uses wild mushrooms, but
you could use ham or bacon instead.

1 Preheat the oven to 180°C/350°F/
Gas 4. Heat the butter in a non-stick
pan and add the mushrooms. Sauté
for 5–7 minutes, or until soft, and
season to taste. Discard any
cooking liquid.

2 Meanwhile, beat the eggs with
the sour cream and cream cheese,
and season to taste. Stir into the
cooked mushroom mixture with
the tarragon.

3 Arrange a pancake in a greased
round cake tin (pan). Spread on a
layer of the mushroom mixture, then
top with another pancake. Continue
in this way until all the pancakes and
filling have been used, finishing with
a pancake.

4 Brush with butter and sprinkle
with the grated cheese. Bake for
30 minutes, or until golden brown.
Serve in wedges, with salad leaves.

PER SERVING: Energy 318kcal/1325kJ; Protein 11g; Carbohydrate 22g, of which sugars 1g; Fat 21g, of which saturates 12g; Cholesterol 162mg; Calcium 179mg; Fibre 2.3g; Sodium 226mg

Serves 4

200g/7oz/1¾ cups plain
    (all-purpose) flour
2 eggs
250ml/8fl oz/1 cup milk
100ml/3½fl oz/scant ½ cup soda
    water
60–75ml/4–5 tbsp clarified butter, or
    olive oil, canola oil or another
    vegetable oil, if preferred
15ml/1 tbsp icing (confectioners') sugar
30ml/2 tbsp chopped walnuts

For the poppy seed filling
75ml/2½fl oz/⅓ cup milk
150g/5oz/1¼ cups poppy seeds
45ml/3 tbsp caster (superfine) sugar
5ml/1 tsp vanilla extract

Poppy Seed Pancakes
Mákos palacsinta

Poppy seeds create a fabulous crunchy texture for the
filling of these fluffy pancakes. You can also add a
handful of poppyseeds to the pancake mixture, so that
their nutty texture infiltrates every part of the dish. Serve
dusted with icing sugar and topped with walnuts.

1 Put the flour, eggs and milk in
a large bowl and whisk to make a
smooth batter. Gradually add the
soda water to make a slightly
thinner consistency, similar to
double (heavy) cream.

2 Heat some of the clarified butter
in a non-stick frying pan and add a
small ladleful of the pancake batter.
Tilt the pan so that the batter covers
the base of the pan and cook for
1 minute on each side, or until
they are golden and crispy – check
by lifting the edge with a metal
spatula to see if it is tinged gold
before turning.

3 Stack them as you make them
between sheets of baking parchment
on a plate over simmering water, to
keep them warm while you cook the
rest. Use the remaining batter to
make eight to ten pancakes.

4 To make the filling, bring the milk
to boiling point, then remove from the
heat. Put the poppy seeds, sugar and
vanilla extract in a bowl and add the
hot milk. Stir well.

5 Fill the pancakes with the poppy
seed filling, fold them, and serve
dusted with icing sugar and sprinkled
with walnuts.

PER SERVING: Energy 504kcal/2112kJ; Protein 20g; Carbohydrate 62g, of which sugars 20g; Fat 42g, of which saturates 13g; Cholesterol 159mg; Calcium 789mg; Fibre 2.2g; Sodium 182mg

Pancakes with Creamy Feta Cheese and Wild Garlic

Sajtos-fokhagymás palacsinta

Here is a classic pancake recipe that can be adapted for any menu, and can be served with various sweet or savoury fillings. Hungarians use soda water in their pancake mixture to make the pancakes beautifully light and fluffy. If you can't find wild garlic, fresh herbs will also taste wonderful with the feta cheese.

Serves 4

200g/7oz/1¾ cups plain (all-purpose) flour
2 eggs
250ml/8fl oz/1 cup milk
100ml/3½fl oz/scant ½ cup soda water
60–75ml/4–5 tbsp clarified butter, or olive oil, canola oil or another vegetable oil, if preferred

For the filling

250g/9oz feta cheese, crumbed
15ml/1 tbsp thick yogurt
100ml/3½fl oz/scant ½ cup sour cream
115g/4oz/4 cups wild garlic leaves, finely chopped
salt and ground black pepper

VARIATION

For a lighter version, substitute the feta cheese for cottage cheese.

1 Put the flour, eggs and milk in a large bowl and whisk to make a smooth batter. Gradually add the soda water to make a slightly thinner consistency, similar to double (heavy) cream.

2 To make the filling, put the feta cheese in a bowl, then add the yogurt, sour cream and wild garlic. Season to taste and mix well to combine.

3 Heat some of the clarified butter in a non-stick frying pan and add a small ladleful of the pancake batter. Tilt the pan so that the batter covers the base of the pan and cook for 1 minute on each side, or until golden and crisp. Lift the edge with a palette knife or metal spatula to see if it is tinged gold before turning. Use the remaining batter to make eight to ten pancakes.

4 Spread some of the cheese, yogurt and sour cream filling in a thin layer over each pancake. Roll each one up and serve.

COOK'S TIPS

• It is advisable to start with a small amount of batter, and then slowly add more batter in the pan if you want to increase the pancake size.
• If you are not sure exactly when to turn the pancake, then pay attention to the bubbles forming and then popping around the edges. When these bubbles pop and the hole does not close up immediately, then the pancake is ready to be turned over.

PER SERVING: Energy 598kcal/2493kJ; Protein 22g; Carbohydrate 48g, of which sugars 6g; Fat 37g, of which saturates 22g; Cholesterol 216mg; Calcium 464mg; Fibre 2.8g; Sodium 1211mg

FISH, MEAT AND GAME

Freshwater fish is a Hungarian favourite, usually served with a strong sauce to balance the forthright flavour and texture of large fish such as carp or pike. The cuisine does, however, focus mainly on meat. All kinds feature on the menu, including beef, chicken, veal and pork, although lamb is a rarity since sheep are kept mainly for their milk and wool. Wild animals in the forests of the western uplands are hunted by those locals who hold permits from the authorities, and this rich resource means that game stews and roasts are often served, particularly of venison.

From fresh water to wild forests

Hungary is a landlocked country, almost as far from the sea as it is possible to get. However, Lake Balaton, in the centre of the western region, supplies local cooks with a fantastic source of zander, a predatory fish which hides in the shallow waters, lying in wait for smaller fish. Pike and carp are also reclusive, preferring calm lake waters and shady corners in which to loiter. The faster-flowing rivers, from the tiny streams flowing down from the Austrian Alps to the wide River Danube, are a good source of salmon and trout. These fish tend to be quite solid and meaty, and their best accompaniment is a sauce flavoured with garden herbs, such as dill, or horseradish. Sour cream and paprika add typical finishing touches.

Poultry recipes vary from simple dishes of chicken breast meat, simmered in a creamy sauce, to more elaborate roasts such as Chicken with Wild Garlic. Here the tasty stuffing mixture is enlivened with dried cherries and wild garlic leaves blended with mustard, breadcrumbs, shallots and walnuts. Chicken and paprika stew (papricas) is one of the signature dishes of Hungarian cuisine.

Main courses in Hungary are often a richer dish of beef, veal or game. Folk memories of herdsmen gathered around an open fire and a tasty one-pot stew still influence the way people cook. Many recipes can be made with different meats, but other ingredients remain the same: vegetables, herbs and spices, particularly paprika. The meat is simmered gently so that it becomes meltingly tender. The finishing touch may be a spoonful of sweet or sour cream stirred into the dish, or a garnish of green (bell) pepper strips or tiny dumplings. Most of these dishes need a good serving of plain rice or potatoes to soak up the delicious juices.

Rabbit is a delicate meat, and is often interchangeable with chicken in recipes. Other game meats are stronger in flavour and colour. Venison has a taste and texture all its own, becoming really succulent when first marinated, then roasted in a herb stock. Wild boar is an even darker meat, and a robust mixture of juniper berries and sharp cherries in the stock transforms the gravy into a delicious sauce. Game meat does not need long cooking – the trick is in the marinade, which makes it tender.

Serves 4

4 pike fillets, 200g/7oz each
30ml/2 tbsp plain (all-purpose) flour
30g/1oz/2½ tbsp butter
45ml/3 tbsp vegetable oil
200g/7oz/2¾ wild mushrooms, cleaned

For the cream and dill sauce

250ml/8fl oz/1 cup fish stock
50ml/2fl oz/¼ cup dry white wine
120ml/4fl oz/½ cup double (heavy) cream
45ml/3 tbsp finely chopped dill
salt and ground black pepper

Pan-fried Pike with Cream and Dill Sauce
Sült csuka kapormártással

Enjoy the subtle taste of pike combined with a delicious dill-flavoured tangy, creamy sauce and earthy-tasting mushrooms. Shallow-frying the pike reduces the amount of fat that is absorbed by the fish meat.

1 Sprinkle the fish with the flour. Heat the butter and oil in a non-stick pan and add the fillets. Cook over medium heat for 2–3 minutes on each side. Add the mushrooms and sauté. Remove the fish and mushrooms and keep hot.

2 To make the sauce, add the stock and wine to the pan, and season. Cook for 5–6 minutes, or until reduced by half. Stir in the cream and dill.

3 Serve each fillet with mushrooms, accompanied by the sauce.

COOK'S TIPS

• Clean and bone the fish while it is fresh.
• Don't let your fish sit in frozen storage longer than necessary. Northern pike don't remain fresh while frozen, so use them within a couple of days.

PER SERVING: Energy 540kcal/2244kJ; Protein 37g; Carbohydrate 7g, of which sugars 1g; Fat 40g, of which saturates 16g; Cholesterol 149mg; Calcium 74mg; Fibre 1.4g; Sodium 491mg

Serves 4

1kg/2¼lb mixed fresh fish (carp, perch,
   eel, trout or other freshwater fish)
2 large onions, roughly chopped
15ml/1 tbsp medium hot paprika
1 red (bell) pepper, cubed
1 tomato, chopped
salt and ground black pepper
bread, to serve

COOK'S TIPS

• Combining different freshwater fish will
increase the soup's aromatic quality.
• For a fish stew it is advisable to use at
least a medium-hot paprika. The
accompanying fresh white bread is
designed to cool the fire of the paprika.

Light Hungarian Fish Stew
Halászlé

Fish stews and soups would traditionally have been
prepared in small kettles on an open fire, mostly by
fishermen themselves. These dishes, prepared with a
mixture of river fish, offered a nutritious and comforting
peasant meal. Every part of Hungary has its own recipe.

1 Remove the head and bones from
the fish and wash them. Cut the flesh
into small pieces and set aside.

2 Put the fish heads and large bones
in a large pan with the onions and
cover with water. Season with salt
and pepper, add the paprika and
bring the mixture to the boil. Simmer
gently for 1 hour.

3 Strain the stock and discard the
solids, then return the stock to the
rinsed pan and add the prepared
pepper, tomato and fish.

4 Cook over low heat for 20 minutes.
Serve with fresh white bread.

PER SERVING: Energy 432kcal/1809kJ; Protein 48g; Carbohydrate 13g, of which sugars 10g; Fat 21g, of which saturates 5g; Cholesterol 271mg; Calcium 85mg; Fibre 2.8g; Sodium 274mg

Serves 4
4 salmon fillets, about 300g/11oz each
30ml/2 tbsp flour
45ml/3 tbsp olive oil
4 egg whites
200ml/7fl oz/scant 1 cup thick natural
　(plain) yogurt
2 egg yolks
small bunch of dill, finely chopped
salt and ground black pepper
green salad, to serve

Salmon with Whipped Yogurt Sauce
Lazac joghurtmártással

The savoury, earthy and slightly sweet taste of salmon is universally appreciated.
Whether farmed or wild, salmon are elegant to look at, light to eat, reliably tasty and
a healthy food choice, being one of the richest sources of beneficial Omega-3 fats.
This dish is simple to prepare, sautéed, then baked, and served to perfection with a
creamy and cleansing yogurt-based sauce.

1 Preheat the oven to 160°C/325°F/
Gas 3. Dust the salmon fillets in the
flour and season with salt and pepper.

2 Heat the olive oil in a non-stick
frying pan. Sauté the salmon
for 2 minutes on each side, or until
cooked though. Remove and arrange
in a flat ovenproof dish.

3 Put the egg whites into a clean,
grease-free bowl and whisk until foamy.

4 Put the yogurt and egg yolks in
another bowl and mix to combine,
then season to taste with salt and
pepper. Add the dill.

5 Fold the egg whites into the egg
yolk mixture and pour over the
salmon. Bake for 10 minutes. Serve
with a green salad.

VARIATION
The recipe can also be prepared with
smoked haddock or cod.

PER SERVING: Energy 749kcal/3118kJ; Protein 69g; Carbohydrate 10g, of which sugars 4g; Fat 49g, of which saturates 9g; Cholesterol 256mg; Calcium 191mg; Fibre 90.3g; Sodium 339mg

Serves 4

20g/³⁄₄oz/¹⁄₂ tbsp butter, for greasing

800g/1³⁄₄lb baby new potatoes, peeled and sliced

800g/1³⁄₄lb cod fillets, cut into chunky pieces

2 bunches of spring onions (scallions), finely chopped

200ml/7fl oz/scant 1 cup sour cream

2.5ml/¹⁄₂ tsp sweet paprika

salt

green salad (optional), to serve

Hungarian Cod Casserole
Tepsis tonhal

The majority of fish used in Hungarian dishes will have been fished from the Danube and Tisza Rivers. While cod is not a freshwater fish and would have been sourced from a coastal fishing port, it did feature on the traditional Hungarian table as a chunky oven-baked casserole, and was a familiar culinary technique for fish. Here it is combined with sour cream, spring onions and, naturally, sweet paprika.

1 Preheat the oven to 150°C/300°F/Gas 2. Butter an oval ovenproof dish and arrange the sliced potatoes over the base, season with salt. Put the pieces of fish on top.

2 Arrange the spring onions on top of the fish. Pour the sour cream over and sprinkle with the paprika. Bake for 40 minutes. Serve with a green salad, if liked.

PER SERVING: Energy 350kcal/1476kJ; Protein 41g; Carbohydrate 34g, of which sugars 4g; Fat 6g, of which saturates 3g; Cholesterol 103mg; Calcium 51mg; Fibre 2.6g; Sodium 2274mg

Serves 4

1kg/2¼lb catfish fillets, cut into chunky
  pieces
30ml/2 tbsp cornflour (cornstarch)
30ml/2 tbsp olive oil
150g/5oz bacon rashers
1 onion, sliced into rings
600g/1lb 6oz sauerkraut
5ml/1 tsp sweet paprika
15ml/1 tbsp tomato purée (paste)
100ml/3½fl oz/scant ½ cup dry white
  wine
salt and ground black pepper

Catfish Fillets with Sauerkraut
Harcsaszeletek savanyú káposztával

Catfish is a popular fish in Hungary and it can be found in just about every lake
and river. Its smooth and succulent white flesh, without bones, is a favourite with
restaurateurs, householders and fishermen alike.

1 Dust the fish with the cornflour
and season with salt and pepper.
Pour the oil into a heavy non-stick
pan and add the bacon. Cook until
crispy, then remove from the pan,
using a slotted spoon.

2 Sauté the fish fillets on both sides
and set aside. Add the onion rings to
the oil in the pan and cook for
2 minutes.

3 Add the sauerkraut, followed by the
paprika and tomato purée, then pour
over the wine, cover and simmer for
15 minutes.

4 Return the crispy bacon to the
pan and arrange the fish on top,
cover and simmer for 2–3 minutes.
Serve the fish accompanied by
the sauerkraut.

COOK'S TIP
Instructions for making sauerkraut are
shown on page 17.

PER SERVING: Energy 471kcal/1966kJ; Protein 53g; Carbohydrate 14g, of which sugars 6g; Fat 21g, of which saturates 4g; Cholesterol 135mg; Calcium 148mg; Fibre 0.9g; Sodium 1814mg

Serves 4

2 large trout, about 600g/1lb 6oz each,
    descaled, gutted and the head removed
2 carrots, sliced
1 parsnip, sliced
1 onion, sliced
juice of $^1/_2$ lemon
300ml/$^1/_2$ pint/1$^1/_4$ cups sour cream
30ml/2 tbsp cornflour (cornstarch)
30ml/2 tbsp creamed horseradish
20g/$^3/_4$oz/$^1/_2$ tbsp butter
salt and ground black pepper
boiled potatoes and steamed green
    vegetables, to serve

Trout in Horseradish Sauce
Pisztráng tejfölös tormával

Trout is one of the favourite freshwater fish abundant in Hungary, along with other varieties such as pike, perch and carp. Horseradish has long been a favourite pairing with fish, and here is deliciously combined with root vegetables, sour cream and the tang of lemon.

1 Cut the fish into small pieces. Put the vegetables and lemon juice into a frying pan and cover with water. Lay the fish on top, then cover and cook for 10 minutes.

2 Meanwhile, combine the sour cream and cornflour in a small pan and stir in the creamed horseradish. Bring to the boil over medium heat. Season to taste with salt and pepper, then add the butter.

3 Add 45–60ml/3–4 tbsp of the fish cooking liquid. Remove the fish from the stock using a slotted spoon and arrange on a serving dish. Pour over the horseradish sauce. Serve with boiled potatoes and lightly steamed green vegetables.

COOK'S TIP
If you don't have a fish scaler, simply use the blunt side of a strong knife. Hold the fish by the tail and scrape from the tail toward the gills 2–3 times.

PER SERVING: Energy 656kcal/2745kJ; Protein 63g; Carbohydrate 22g, of which sugars 11g; Fat 36g, of which saturates 15g; Cholesterol 258mg; Calcium 164mg; Fibre 3.2g; Sodium 381mg

Chicken Stuffed with Wild Garlic

Fokhagymás töltött csirke

The stuffing is the integral element to this recipe, with the mixed flavours of walnuts, cherries, wine and mustard combining and infiltrating the chicken as it roasts in the oven. Töltött csirke is also delicious when served cold.

Serves 4
1.5kg/3¼lb free-range chicken
15ml/1 tbsp olive oil

For the stuffing
a small knob (pat) of butter
1 shallot, finely chopped
60ml/4 tbsp walnuts, chopped
115g/4oz/1 cup dried cherries
100ml/3½fl oz/scant ½ cup dry
  white wine
2 slices white bread, processed into
  breadcrumbs
10ml/2 tsp wholegrain mustard
115g/4oz/4 cups wild garlic leaves
salt and ground black pepper
potatoes or rice, braised or steamed
  vegetables and salad, to serve

1 Preheat the oven to 200°C/400°F/Gas 6. To make the stuffing, melt the butter in a medium pan and cook the shallot and walnuts over low heat for 3 minutes, or until the shallot is soft.

2 Add the cherries and wine, and cook until the wine has almost evaporated. Stir in the breadcrumbs, mustard and wild garlic leaves, mixing well. Season to taste.

3 Spoon the stuffing into the cavity of the chicken, then put in a roasting pan. Brush all over the chicken with the oil. Roast for 30 minutes, then reduce the temperature to 180°C/350°F/Gas 4, and continue cooking for another hour, basting every now and then with the cooking juices.

4 Test that the chicken is cooked by piercing the thickest part of the leg with the point of a knife; the juices should run clear and the flesh should be white, not pink. Leave to rest before serving. Serve with potatoes or rice, vegetables and salad.

COOK'S TIPS

• Wait to stuff the chicken until just before it is to be cooked – the reduces the risk of bacterial growth. First, scald the chicken inside and out and pat the skin dry with a paper towel. Stuff the chicken through the neck, into the body cavities, but not too tightly because the stuffing expands as the chicken cooks.

• Wild garlic grows in moist ground under dappled shade. The leaves should be harvested in the spring before the plant flowers. The leaves and flowers of wild garlic should be washed thoroughly before cooking.

• Wild garlic has the added benefit of reducing cholesterol and high blood pressure – what is more, the juices in its leaves have antiseptic qualities.

VARIATION

For a more intense flavour, add a selection of fresh green herbs such as chives, basil, mint and parsley as you cook the shallot and walnuts in step one.

PER SERVING: Energy 516kcal/2149kJ; Protein 29g; Carbohydrate 23g, of which sugars 14g; Fat 33g, of which saturates 7g; Cholesterol 115mg; Calcium 120mg; Fibre 4.4g; Sodium 434mg

Chicken and Paprika Stew with Sour Cream
Paprikás-tejfölös csirkepörkölt

Papricas, pronounced 'papricash', is another traditional stew typical of Hungary. It is always made with lean meat – veal, chicken or rabbit – and cooked with sour cream. It is likely to become a family favourite at mealtimes, and this recipe is well tried and tested, prepared in homes and restaurants since the end of the 18th century.

Serves 6

45ml/3 tbsp vegetable oil
1 onion, chopped
5ml/1 tsp sweet paprika
4 large skinless chicken breast fillets, cut into 2.5cm/1in cubes
2 large tomatoes, cubed
2 green (bell) peppers, seeded and thinly sliced
300ml/¹⁄₂ pint/1¹⁄₄ cups sour cream
10ml/2 tsp plain (all-purpose) flour
salt and ground black pepper

1 Heat the oil in a heavy pan and cook the onion until just golden. Remove from the heat and add the paprika, stirring well.

2 Return the pan to the heat and add the chicken, 50ml/2fl oz/¹⁄₄ cup water and the tomatoes. Season with salt and pepper, mix well, then cover and cook for 15 minutes, adding a little more water if necessary.

3 Remove the lid and continue cooking over low heat for 15 minutes more. Add the sliced green peppers and stir well.

4 Combine two-thirds of the sour cream with the flour, if using, and add to the sauce.

5 Cook over a low heat for 5–7 minutes, then serve the stew with a dollop of the remaining sour cream.

COOK'S TIPS
• Paprika, as with other spices that have been ground, will lose its potency over time, so aim to use it within six months. When buying paprika, choose a tin container rather than a glass bottle because light will damage the spice. Store paprika in an airtight container in a cool, dark place, ideally the refrigerator.
• Paprika has been found to be a rich source of vitamin C and beta-carotene.

PER SERVING: Energy 309kcal/1288kJ; Protein 27g; Carbohydrate 8g, of which sugars 6g; Fat 19g, of which saturates 8g; Cholesterol 100mg; Calcium 69mg; Fibre 2.1g; Sodium 154mg

Serves 4
50g/2oz/¼ cup butter
1 onion, chopped
5ml/1 tsp sweet paprika
115g/4oz smoked bacon,
   cubed
2 green (bell) peppers,
   chopped
200g/7oz/2¾ cups wild
   mushrooms, sliced
1 tomato, chopped
150g/5oz/1¹/₂ cups peas
100ml/3¹/₂fl oz/scant ¹/₂ cup
   veal stock
15ml/1 tbsp olive oil
4 fillet steaks (beef tenderloins)
   (200g/7oz each)
salt and ground black pepper
rice, to serve

Hussar Beef
Marhaszelet huszár módra

Fillet of beef is associated with a lack of visible fat and a tender texture. This name refers to the Hussars, who rode with cuts of beef beneath their saddles to tenderize them.

1 Melt the butter in a large, heavy non-stick pan over low heat and add the onion. Add the paprika and the bacon and cook for 5 minutes.

2 Add the green peppers, mushrooms, tomato and peas. Season to taste and add the veal stock. Cook over high heat for 5 minutes, then reduce to a simmer for another 10 minutes, or until the liquid has almost evaporated.

3 Pour the oil into a non-stick frying pan and add the beef. Season with salt and pepper, and cook for 4–5 minutes on each side for medium. Serve the beef fillet accompanied by the vegetable mixture and boiled rice.

COOK'S TIP
Beef tenderloin is the roast cut from the centre of the tenderloin – it is best eaten with a pink centre. Over-cooking a beef fillet will make it dry and tasteless.

VARIATION
Use lamb or chicken for a lighter option.

PER SERVING: Energy 539kcal/2249kJ; Protein 52g; Carbohydrate 10g, of which sugars 0g; Fat33g, of which saturates 15g; Cholesterol 168mg; Calcium 46mg; Fibre 6.1g; Sodium 732mg

Serves 4

400g/14oz thin veal escalopes
  (US veal scallops)
40g/1½oz/3 tbsp butter
1 large shallot, finely chopped
400g/14oz/5½ cups button (white)
  mushrooms, finely chopped
5ml/1 tsp plain (all-purpose) flour
120ml/4fl oz/½ cup sour cream
120ml/4fl oz/½ cup veal stock
60ml/4 tbsp dry white wine
salt and ground black pepper
boiled potatoes, to serve

Veal and Mushroom Fricassée
Gombás borjúbecsinált

This light braise with a velvety sauce is much loved by Hungarians. Veal escalopes are tender cuts that are normally made from the fillet end of the leg. The recipe can use chicken or pork instead of the veal, or, for a vegetarian option, double the quantity of mushrooms.

1 Beat the veal escalopes very thinly between clear film (plastic wrap) or baking parchment (or ask your butcher to do it for you), as you would for a schnitzel. Slice into thin strips.

2 Heat a third of the butter in a heavy non-stick pan over medium heat. Add the shallot and sauté until soft, and then add the mushrooms, cooking them until lightly browned. The mushrooms will release some liquid, so cook until this liquid has evaporated. Remove the mushroom mixture from the pan and set aside until needed.

3 Melt half the remaining butter in the same pan and gently sauté the veal strips for 5 minutes.

4 In a pan, melt the remaining butter and sprinkle in the flour, stirring constantly. Very slowly, add the sour cream and veal stock, stirring constantly. Season, then continue cooking over low-medium heat until the sauce has thickened.

PER SERVING: Energy 262kcal/1093kJ; Protein 24g; Carbohydrate 3g, of which sugars 2g; Fat 16g, of which saturates 10g; Cholesterol 91mg; Calcium 41mg; Fibre 0.3g; Sodium 273mg

Veal Croquettes
Borjúfasírt

These mouthwatering croquettes provide a tasty light lunch or a more substantial evening meal. The walnuts and raisins give a layered texture to the stuffing of the veal discs, which are then quickly fried before developing a crusty shell during a short spell in the oven.

Serves 4
2 slices white bread
100ml/3½fl oz/scant ½ cup milk
500g/1¼lb veal, minced (ground)
75ml/5 tbsp finely chopped fresh parsley
1 large egg
vegetable oil, for shallow frying
200g/7oz/3½ cups brioche breadcrumbs
salt and ground black pepper
For the stuffing
30ml/2 tbsp of vegetable oil
1 small onion, finely chopped
115g/4oz/1 cup walnuts, chopped
115g/4oz/scant 1 cup raisins
1.5ml/¼ tsp ground cumin
1.5ml/¼ tsp ground cinnamon

1 Preheat the oven to 180°C/350°F/Gas 4. Soak the bread in the milk for 5 minutes. Gently squeeze out the excess milk, and break the bread into small pieces.

2 Put the bread into a medium bowl, add the veal mince, parsley and egg, and season with salt and pepper. Mix well to combine.

3 To make the stuffing, heat the oil in a large frying pan and sauté the onion for 3 minutes. Add the walnuts and allow them to gently brown, then add the raisins, cumin and cinnamon, and simmer gently for another 5 minutes. Remove from the heat.

4 Take a small handful of the veal mixture and form into a flat disc. Put a tablespoonful of the walnut stuffing in the centre and wrap the edges around it, rolling it into a largish meatball. Gently form an oval croquette. Repeat with the remaining veal mixture and stuffing.

5 Put the oil for shallow frying into a frying pan. Roll the croquettes in the brioche crumbs and fry gently for 3 minutes on each side to brown. Transfer to an ovenproof dish and cook in the oven for 15 minutes. Serve hot, with a crisp green salad.

COOK'S TIP
• Mini-croquettes can also be fun, in which case, mould smaller shapes from the veal mixture.
• When you fry the croquettes, ensure that they are not touching and keep rolling them in the oil.
• Depending on the size of your pan, you might need to cook the croquettes in batches.
• While these croquettes don't use vegetables, it is an excellent method of using up unused cooked vegetables, combined with the meat or on their own.

PER SERVING: Energy 518kcal/2158kJ; Protein 13g; Carbohydrate 39g, of which sugars 5g; Fat 36g, of which saturates 5g; Cholesterol 67mg; Calcium 161mg; Fibre 2.4g; Sodium 490mg

Transylvanian Venison Stew
Erdélyi szarvaspörkölt

This is a stew from the region of Transylvania in the Carpathian Basin, which was ruled by the Hungarians for many centuries after the Magyar invasion in the 7th century. Its base is always formed with oil, onions and paprika. This version is made with venison, but beef and mutton can also be used. The meat should always be cut into short, thin slices and not cubes, as would be the case for a goulash. It is a delightfully quick stew to prepare.

Serves 4
15ml/1 tbsp vegetable oil
1 onion, finely chopped
800g/1¾lb venison leg, cut into thin strips
1 garlic clove, crushed
200ml/7fl oz/scant 1 cup white wine
10ml/2 tsp tomato purée (paste)
5ml/1 tsp sweet paprika
salt and ground black pepper
mashed potatoes, to serve

1 Heat the oil in a flameproof casserole, then fry the onion for 3–4 minutes. Add the venison strips and brown in the casserole for 4–5 minutes. Season to taste with salt and pepper.

2 Add the garlic and white wine, and simmer, covered, over a low heat for about 20 minutes.

3 Add the tomato purée and paprika. Stir gently and cover, then cook for a further 30 minutes, or until the meat is soft and tender. The sauce will have thickened by the end of cooking. Serve with mashed potatoes.

VARIATION
If you prefer, use lean steak of beef instead of the pork tenderloin.

COOK'S TIP
• If you use a piece of boned meat, then you can pull out the meat and remove the bones after simmering for 20 minutes.
• If you are not set on venison, look for stewing meat when purchasing the ingredients, such as flesh that has been trimmed away from roasts or chops. Tougher pieces of pork and beef will tenderize when they are cooked slowly.
• If you are preparing meat from a venison carcass for a stew, save the meatiest part of the hind legs for steak meat (cut a line close to the bone, take the meat away and carve the steaks by cutting from the outside of the meat to the bone). Then cut the remaining meat on the hind legs and the meat from the front leg bones into strips.

PER SERVING: Energy 291kcal/1227kJ; Protein 45g; Carbohydrate 4g, of which sugars 3g; Fat 8g, of which saturates 2g; Cholesterol 100mg; Calcium 26mg; Fibre 0.6g; Sodium 218mg

Serves 4

400g/14oz coarsely minced (ground)
  venison
200g/7oz minced (ground) veal
1 onion, finely chopped
45ml/3 tbsp breadcrumbs
5–6 oregano sprigs, finely chopped
1 egg, beaten
5ml/3 tbsp plain (all-purpose) flour, for
  dusting
60ml/4 tbsp olive oil
2.5ml/$\frac{1}{2}$ tsp sweet paprika
100ml/3$\frac{1}{2}$fl oz/scant $\frac{1}{2}$ cup chicken stock
45ml/3 tbsp sour cream
a handful of fresh herbs, leaves chopped
salt and ground black pepper

Venison Meatballs
Szarvas-húsgombóc

After preparing an initial meal of venison, any unused
pieces can be minced (ground) to make delicious
meatballs, served in a sour cream sauce. You can
use other meats, perhaps wild boar, beef or veal.

1 Put the venison and veal in a bowl
with the onion, and season with salt
and pepper.

2 Add the breadcrumbs, oregano and
egg to the bowl, and mix them well
to combine.

3 Shape the meat mixture into
meatballs and dust with the flour.

4 Fry the meatballs over medium
heat for 12–15 minutes, turning to
cook evenly. Remove and keep warm.

5 Add the paprika, followed by the
chicken stock. Bring to the boil, then
simmer until reduced by half.

6 Add the sour cream and fresh herbs.
Pour over the meatballs and serve.

PER SERVING: Energy 383kcal/1608kJ; Protein 38g; Carbohydrate 21g, of which sugars 3g; Fat 18g, of which saturates 5g; Cholesterol 146mg; Calcium 79mg; Fibre 1.9g; Sodium 351mg

Serves 4
30ml/2 tbsp vegetable oil
1 onion, finely chopped
1kg/2¼lb rabbit pieces
5ml/1 tsp sweet paprika
3 green (bell) peppers, thinly sliced
2 ripe tomatoes, chopped
200ml/7fl oz/scant 1 cup chicken stock
1 extra green (bell) pepper, sliced thinly,
    to garnish
sautéed potatoes, rice or dumplings,
    to serve
salt and ground black pepper

Rabbit Goulash Stew
Nyúlpörkölt

A traditional Hungarian goulash has the texture of a soup. This goulash stew has a much thicker sauce. It can be served as a hearty main course, accompanied by potatoes, rice or dumplings. Pörkölt-style dishes can also be made using pork or beef.

1 Heat the oil in to a heavy flameproof casserole dish. Fry the onion with the rabbit pieces. Season to taste with salt and pepper.

2 Add the paprika, the green peppers and the tomatoes, and stir the mixture to combine.

3 Add the chicken stock, then cover and simmer for 1 hour, or until the meat is cooked through and tender.

4 When ready to serve, lay the green pepper slices for the garnish over the top of the stew and serve with sautéed potatoes, rice or any dumplings of your choice.

COOK'S TIPS
• Wild rabbit is leaner than tame rabbit, but does have a gamey quality. This can be reduced by soaking the meat in salted water overnight.
• Ask your butcher to cut the rabbit into smallish pieces. You can also buy selected pieces from the legs or thigh.

PER SERVING: Energy 229kcal/957kJ; Protein 24g; Carbohydrate 8g, of which sugars 6g; Fat 12g, of which saturates 3g; Cholesterol 86mg; Calcium 64mg; Fibre 3.4g; Sodium 243mg

Fricassée of Rabbit and Prunes
Nyúlbecsinált szilvával

Hungary's production of rabbit meat is second only to France. While not among the core ingredients used in the Hungarian kitchen, many people like this distinctive meat that is high in protein and lower in cholesterol and fat than chicken, beef or pork. This fricassée throws a mélange of flavourful vegetables, along with eggs and cream, into the mix, with the unexpectedly delightful final addition of prunes.

Serves 4

2 rabbits, chopped into portions
1 onion, chopped
30ml/2 tbsp olive oil
2 leeks, white part only, sliced
2 carrots, sliced
2 celery sticks, sliced
100ml/3½fl oz/scant ½ cup dry
   white wine
300ml/½ pint/1¼ cups chicken stock
10 cloves
2 parsley sprigs
5 fresh bay leaves
50g/2oz/¼ cup butter
30ml/2 tbsp plain (all-purpose) flour
3 egg yolks
120ml/4fl oz/½ cup single (light) cream
30ml/2 tbsp chopped fresh thyme leaves
115g/4oz/½ cup prunes, stoned (pitted)
   and sliced
salt and ground black pepper
rice, to serve

1 Preheat the oven to 160°C/325°F/Gas 3. Cut the rabbit into quarters. In a heavy flameproof casserole, brown the onion in the olive oil, then add the leeks, carrots and celery, and sauté for 5 minutes.

2 Arrange the rabbit pieces over the vegetables, then pour in the wine and chicken stock. Add the cloves, parsley and bay leaves, and season with salt and pepper.

3 Put the casserole in the oven and cook for 1½ hours, or until the rabbit is tender. Take out of the oven and keep warm. Pour out the cooking liquid and keep it in reserve.

4 In a shallow pan, melt the butter, then add the flour and cook until light brown. Gradually add most of the cooking liquid, stirring until the sauce is thick and smooth. Mix the egg yolks and cream together in a bowl and add them to the sauce. Simmer gently – do not allow it to boil.

5 Add the thyme and prunes to the sauce, then pour into the casserole dish with the rabbit. Return to the heat and simmer for 2–3 minutes, then serve with plain boiled rice.

PER SERVING: Energy 588kcal/2452kJ; Protein 44g; Carbohydrate 24g, of which sugars 17g; Fat 34g, of which saturates 15g; Cholesterol 341mg; Calcium 174mg; Fibre 6.9g; Sodium 302mg

Goulash Puff Pies

Leveles tésztában sütött pörkölt

Puff pastry would always have been prepared by hand in the traditional Hungarian kitchen, but modern cooks should settle with the easily available pre-prepared chilled or frozen versions. Such pies might originally have been made to use up leftover gulyás, but this recipe explains how to prepare fresh gulyás if that is more convenient. Beef fillet is used here, but cheaper cuts of meat can be used. You will need six single-portion ovenproof dishes to make these mouthwatering pies.

Serves 6

200g/7oz puff pastry, thawed
   if frozen
1 egg yolk, beaten
sour cream, to serve

For the filling

800g/1¾lb fillet steak (beef tenderloin),
   cut into 2.5cm/1in cubes
15ml/1 tbsp cornflour (cornstarch)
60ml/4 tbsp olive oil
1 onion, thinly sliced
2 garlic cloves, crushed
2.5ml/½ tsp caraway seeds
10ml/2 tsp sweet paprika
100ml/3½fl oz/scant ½ cup beef stock
400g/14oz can chopped tomatoes
30ml/2 tbsp chopped fresh oregano
   leaves
salt and ground black pepper

COOK'S TIPS

• If you decide to make a large single pie for this dish, then increase the cooking time by at least 10 minutes.
• Always select the best steak, as the pies need so little cooking.

1 Preheat the oven to 200°C/400°F/Gas 6. To make the filling, put the beef and cornflour in a large bowl and mix well to coat the beef pieces. Season with salt and pepper.

2 Heat half the oil in a large, heavy frying pan and sauté the coated beef, a few cubes at a time, so that they can be browned evenly without being crowded in the pan. When all the meat has been browned, remove to one side.

3 Add the remaining oil to the pan with the onion, garlic and caraway seeds, stirring constantly. Remove from the heat and add the paprika, stirring well, then return the pan to the stove to continue cooking. Add the beef, stock and tomatoes, and simmer uncovered for about 50 minutes, or until the cooking juices have reduced by half. Add the oregano and leave it to cool completely.

4 Roll the pastry to 5mm/¼in thick and cut out six large circles about 12–15cm/4½–6in in diameter, or to cover the tops of your individual pie dishes.

5 Spoon the goulash into six individual pie dishes and put the pastry rounds over each, pressing the sides down to seal well. Cut a cross in the top of each pastry topping and brush with egg yolk.

6 Bake the pies for 30 minutes, or until the tops are golden in colour. Serve with sour cream.

PER SERVING: Energy 444kcal/1852kJ; Protein 32g; Carbohydrate 19g, of which sugars 4g; Fat 28g, of which saturates 5g; Cholesterol 155mg; Calcium 48mg; Fibre 1.7g; Sodium 285mg

Serves 4
200g/7oz bacon, cubed
½ leg venison
1 large carrot, sliced
1 parsnip, sliced
1 onion, sliced
3 garlic cloves, finely sliced
8 peppercorns
5ml/1 tsp baby capers
2 bay leaves
200ml/7fl oz/scant 1 cup dry white wine
mashed potato, to serve

Roast Leg of Venison in White Wine and Pepper Sauce

Szarvascomb borsos fehérbormártással

This recipe coats the joint with cubed bacon to maintain the moisture in the joint and add enormous flavour. Getting good-quality meat, preferably from a younger deer, will ensure the best results. You can ask your butcher to tunnel-bone the joint for you – this removes the leg bones but keeps the meat intact.

1 Preheat the oven to 200°C/400°F/ Gas 6. Cook the bacon in a non-stick pan until it is browned. Remove from the heat.

2 Put the venison into an ovenproof dish and pour over the cooked bacon with its fat.

3 Add the carrot, parsnip and onion to the dish together with the garlic, peppercorns, capers and bay leaves.

4 Add 100ml/3½fl oz/scant ½ cup water and the white wine, then put in the oven and cook for 1 hour, or 1½ hours if you prefer your venison well done.

5 Rest the meat for 20 minutes before carving. Slice and serve with some of the sauce, accompanied by mashed potato.

PER SERVING: Energy 463/1953kJ; Protein 76g; Carbohydrate 10g, of which sugars 6g; Fat 15g, of which saturates 6g; Cholesterol 177mg; Calcium 48mg; Fibre 2.7g; Sodium 945mg

Serves 4

150g/5oz bacon, cubed

1 large onion, chopped

2 garlic cloves, crushed

500g/1¼lb diced venison shoulder

1 cup water, or enough to cover
  ingredients

5ml/1 tsp sweet paprika

2.5ml/½ tsp caraway seeds

15ml/1 tbsp dried marjoram

200g/7oz/2¾ cups wild mushrooms,
  cleaned

1 carrot, peeled and sliced

1 parsnip, peeled and sliced

800ml/27fl oz/scant 3¼ cups chicken
  stock

1 sliced green (bell) pepper and crusty
  bread, to serve

Venison Goulash

Gombás szarvasgulyás

This is a variation of the classic Hungarian gulyás, a meat and vegetable stew that was traditionally prepared with beef, veal, pork or lamb by cattle or sheep herders. One of many gulyás recipes, this one with venison would have been a favourite at mealtimes throughout the hunting season.

1 Put the bacon into a large pan and cook over medium heat.

2 Add the onion, garlic and venison to the pan and cover the ingredients with the water. Cover and cook over low heat for 1 hour, stirring from time to time.

3 Add the paprika, caraway seeds and marjoram, along with the wild mushrooms, carrot and green pepper.

4 Pour over the stock, then cover and simmer gently for 20–30 minutes, until the meat is tender. Serve with sliced green pepper and crusty bread.

PER SERVING: Energy 282kcal/1186kJ; Protein 37g; Carbohydrate 13g, of which sugars 8g; Fat 10g, of which saturates 4g; Cholesterol 82mg; Calcium 60mg; Fibre 4.9g; Sodium 947mg

Hunter's-style Roasted Venison

Szarvassült vadász módra

During the hunting season this dish will be served regularly as a centrepiece. The joint is marinated for two days, and the venison is traditionally served with braised red cabbage with caraway seeds and sautéed potatoes.

Serves 8

2kg/4½lb leg of venison
30ml/2 tbsp vegetable oil
10 streaky (fatty) bacon rashers (strips)
100ml/3½fl oz/scant ½ cup sour cream
a handful of mixed fresh herbs, such as
    parsley, tarragon and rosemary
salt and ground black pepper

For the marinade

45ml/3 tbsp white wine vinegar
90ml/6 tbsp olive oil
10 green peppercorns
2 bay leaves
6 juniper berries
2.5ml/½ tsp dried mixed herbs
grated juice and rind of 1 lemon
1 carrot, chopped
1 leek, chopped
1 onion chopped
2 garlic cloves, crushed

COOK'S TIP

You can keep fresh game frozen for up to 8 months. If you freeze seasoned or cured game, keep it for up to 4 months.

VARIATION

Prepare this dish using a rack of venison – marinade in the same way as above, and reduce the cooking time.

1 To make the marinade, put the vinegar, olive oil, peppercorns, bay leaves, juniper berries, mixed herbs, lemon juice and rind, carrot, leek, onion and garlic in a pan. Season to taste with salt and pepper and bring to the boil, then simmer for 15 minutes. Pour into a large bowl and leave to cool.

2 Add the venison, and rub all over with the marinade, then cover with clear film (plastic wrap) and chill for 48 hours.

3 When ready to cook, preheat the oven to 180°C/350°F/Gas 4. Remove the venison from the marinade. Heat the oil and sauté the venison on all sides until golden. Season with salt and pepper.

4 Put the venison in a roasting pan and lay the bacon rashers over it. Pour the marinade around the meat and add 150ml/¼ pint/⅔ cup water.

5 Cover with foil and cook in a preheated oven for 30 minutes. Remove the foil and continue cooking for 55 minutes or until cooked through but still pink. If you prefer your meat well done, cook for 5–10 minutes longer. Remove from the oven and allow to rest for 20 minutes.

6 Pour the cooking juices into a small pan and bring to the boil, then simmer and add the sour cream. Mix well and add the herbs.

7 Remove the venison from the heat. Carve the meat and serve with the sour cream sauce.

PER SERVING: Energy 401kcal/1678kJ; Protein 62g; Carbohydrate 0g, of which sugars 0g; Fat18g, of which saturates 6g; Cholesterol 155mg; Calcium 26mg; Fibre 0.0g; Sodium 563mg

Wild Boar with Juniper Berries and Sour Cherry Sauce

Borókás vaddisznósült meggyszósszal

Hunting always was, and still is, a passion for the Hungarian people, and they take great pride in preparing intensely flavoured game dishes. Here, the robust wild boar contrasts nicely with the sweet-and-sour flavour of the sauce. The flavoursome meat is prepared with a juniper marinade. This recipe also works well using beef fillet.

Serves 6

6 wild boar fillets, about 150g/5oz each, rolled and tied with string
60ml/4 tbsp olive oil
salt and ground black pepper

For the marinade

200ml/7fl oz/scant 1 cup red wine
4–6 thyme sprigs
4–6 rosemary sprigs
1 garlic clove, crushed
1 small shallot, finely chopped
1 small carrot, finely chopped
1 celery stalk, finely chopped
8 white peppercorns
10 juniper berries, crushed

For the sauce

20g/³/₄oz/¹/₂ tbsp butter
300g/11oz/scant 2 cups fresh or frozen cherries, pitted
10ml/2 tsp redcurrant jelly
2.5ml/¹/₂ tsp chopped fresh thyme
100ml/3¹/₂fl oz/scant ¹/₂ cup veal or good chicken stock

1 Put all the marinade ingredients in a large dish. Mix well and then put the wild boar fillets into the marinade to infuse (steep) for 2 hours.

2 Preheat the oven to 200°C/400°F/Gas 6. When ready to cook the wild boar fillet, lift out of the marinade, and dry well; reserve the marinade. Lightly brush the meat with some of the oil, and season with salt and pepper.

3 Seal the mini joints in a large frying pan in the remaining oil, caramelizing them on all sides.

4 Transfer the mini joints to an ovenproof dish and cook in the preheated oven for 10–12 minutes until just pink, or longer if you like your meat medium to well done. Rest the meat for 5–10 minutes.

5 Meanwhile, to make the sauce, melt the butter in a heavy pan and sauté the vegetables from the marinade, reserving the liquid. Add the cherries, redcurrant jelly, thyme and half the marinade liquor with the stock. Cook over medium heat until reduced by half, then pass through a fine sieve (strainer), and season. Keep warm and rest before carving.

6 Slice the fillets horizontally into five. Arrange the slices of wild boar on serving plates, and pour around the sour cherry sauce.

PER SERVING: Energy 353kcal/1472kJ; Protein 32g; Carbohydrate 7g, of which sugars 7g; Fat 22g, of which saturates 7g; Cholesterol 99mg; Calcium 14mg; Fibre 0.8g; Sodium 180mg.

DESSERTS AND BAKING

Most Hungarian sweet dishes date only from the last 150 years. These mouthwatering morsels of pastry, sponge cake, chocolate, nuts and fruit were not known to the Magyars sitting round their fires on the Great Hungarian Plain. It was the prosperity of the 19th century that saw coffee houses springing up in Budapest and other cities, and these sold a variety of sweet cakes. Of the ingredients, only the fruit and nuts are native to Hungary, while filo pastry arrived with the Turks, and the way of transforming it into apple strudel was an Austrian invention.

Flaky pastry and fruit fillings

The majority of the sweet baked goods so beloved of Hungarians can either be served for dessert or eaten as a snack. There is very little difference between the two, especially as the cakes and strudels are usually so soft that they have to be eaten with a fork or spoon.

The aromatic flavour of poppy seeds permeates many of these recipes. These are an acquired taste, but a truly traditional Hungarian one. In fact, these tiny black seeds are favourites in most central European countries, particularly in celebration cakes for Christmas and Easter. In one recipe in this section, they are sprinkled on top of little individual filo rolls packed with a bland cottage cheese filling. The classic Hungarian blurring of the boundaries between sweet and savoury flavours comes to the fore here, as the filo rolls are neither sweet nor savoury, and the taste of this dish is all in the added ingredients – black pepper, poppy seeds and honey. A sweeter strudel recipe with poppy seeds uses the seeds both in the filling and as a topping. They are ground finely to flavour the apple inside the strudel, and left whole to decorate the outside.

Stone fruits, such as cherries, plums and apricots, and orchard fruits, such as apples and pears, grow well in the Hungarian climate, and fill many a cake, pancake or pie. Often the simplest recipes, such as roasted pears, just need the addition of a Hungarian twist, and here that twist consists of rosemary, balsamic vinegar and honey. Fruits also combine beautifully with nuts, and there are several recipes for desserts and cakes made with fragrant almonds and raspberries or cherries. Chocolate is a natural partner to nuts, and the recipe here for chocolate almond torte is a wonderfully light confection, with the dark chocolate blended with cream.

The classic cake served in every Hungarian household over the Christmas period is a pastry dish made with sweetened shortcrust pastry rather than filo pastry, which makes it more substantial. Fresh fruit would naturally be in short supply at this time of year, so the traditional Hungarian Christmas loaf is stuffed with shiny dried fruit and nuts, just a pinch of sweet cinnamon and vanilla and a citrus tang combining for a wonderful Christmassy aroma.

Serves 4
2 large slightly under-ripe pears
30ml/2 tbsp butter
leaves from 3 rosemary sprigs
45ml/3 tbsp balsamic vinegar
60ml/4 tbsp clear honey

Roasted Pears with Honey
Sült mézes körte

This dish is a perfect demonstration of the combination of traditional and modern cooking, a trend that is becoming increasingly evident on the culinary scene in Hungary. The flavour of the caramelized balsamic vinegar works beautifully with the savoury rosemary and sweet intonations of the pears and honey.

1 Preheat the oven to 200°C/400°F/ Gas 6. Halve and core the pears, but do not peel them.

2 Melt the butter in a heavy pan that can be used in the oven. When just beginning to bubble, add the pears, cut sides down. Add the rosemary leaves, then sauté for 2 minutes. Transfer the pan to the preheated oven and roast for 20 minutes.

3 Add the vinegar and roast for a further 5 minutes. Remove the pan from the oven and drizzle with honey. Leave the pears to rest and then serve them warm.

PER SERVING: Energy 151kcal/635kJ; Protein 1g; Carbohydrate 24g, of which sugars 24g; Fat 6g, of which saturates 4g; Cholesterol 16mg; Calcium 16mg; Fibre 0g; Sodium 51mg

Serves 6
24 plump ready-to-eat prunes, pitted
juice of 1 orange
5ml/1 tsp plain (all-purpose) flour
60ml/4 tbsp sour cream
grated rind of 1 orange
45ml/3 tbsp brioche breadcrumbs
30ml/2 tbsp ground walnuts
50g/2oz/¼ cup butter, cubed

Walnut Baked Prunes

Diós-szilvás morzsa

Hungary provides perfect growing conditions for plums, known as szilvás, and the country is one of the world's major producers. Unsurprisingly, therefore, Hungarians love plums, and when in season they preserve them or dry them for the winter months. This is a traditional, simple winter dessert using prunes.

1 Preheat the oven to 160°C/325°F/ Gas 3. Put the prunes in a pan with the orange juice and 200ml/7fl oz/ scant 1 cup water, and simmer for 5 minutes over medium heat.

2 Remove the prunes with a slotted spoon and bring the liquid to the boil. Cook for 10 minutes, or until reduced by half.

3 Mix the flour and sour cream to make a smooth paste and mix into the reduced liquid. Simmer together for 5 minutes.

4 Arrange the prunes in a shallow, greased baking tray and pour over the sour cream mixture. Sprinkle with the orange rind, brioche breadcrumbs and walnuts. Dot with butter cubes. Bake for 20–25 minutes, or until golden. Serve hot or cold.

COOK'S TIPS
• To stone prunes, cut a slit in them with a sharp knife and push the pit out.
• To rehydrate prunes, cover them with water in a pan and simmer for 10 minutes.

PER SERVING: Energy 166kcal/698kJ; Protein 3g; Carbohydrate 22g, of which sugars 17g; Fat 8g, of which saturates 2g; Cholesterol 6mg; Calcium 41mg; Fibre 6.5g; Sodium 49mg

Apricot Pie
Sárgabarackos pite

Apricots are much loved throughout Hungary. They are eaten fresh when in season, as they are or used in desserts, and preserved in jars for the winter months as compotes. Apples, plums or pears also taste very good indeed in this traditional Hungarian pie.

Serves 8

250g/9oz/generous 1 cup very cold butter, cubed, plus extra for greasing
500g/1¼lb/5 cups plain (all-purpose) flour
130g/4½oz caster (superfine) sugar
1 egg yolk
30ml/2 tbsp sour cream
1 small egg, beaten, for brushing
60ml/4 tbsp chopped almonds

For the filling

2kg/4½lb fresh apricots, stones (pits) removed, cubed
45ml/3 tbsp soft light brown sugar
30ml/2 tbsp ground almonds

1 Put the butter into a bowl and add the flour. Using your fingertips, rub the flour into the butter until it resembles fine breadcrumbs.

2 Add the sugar, egg yolk and sour cream, and work the dough until it is completely smooth. Chill, covered, for 2 hours.

3 Preheat the oven to 180°C/350°F/Gas 4 and butter a 20cm/8in, shallow, square cake tin (pan). To make the filling, put the apricots and brown sugar into a large bowl and mix together well.

4 Remove the dough from the refrigerator and divide it in half. Roll each half to about 5mm/¼in thickness.

5 Line the cake tin with one of the rolled dough pieces. Sprinkle with the ground almonds and then spoon in the apricots.

6 Moisten the edge of the pastry with water, then cover with the remaining dough and seal all the edges. Prick the pie top with a fork. Brush with beaten egg and sprinkle with the chopped almonds. Bake the pie for 40 minutes, or until golden brown. Cool completely before serving.

COOK'S TIPS
• When buying apricots, look for plump and juicy ones with an evenly distributed orange colour. Mature fruit will respond to gentle pressure on the skin.
• To encourage immature apricots to ripen, put the fruit in a paper bag with an apple.
• Apricots can be frozen for up to a year – cut the fruit into halves, place on a flat tray and freeze them. Once frozen, transfer them to a plastic freezer bag.

PER SERVING: Energy 599kcal/2515kJ; Protein 11g; Carbohydrate 73g, of which sugars 25g; Fat 32g, of which saturates 18g; Cholesterol 121mg; Calcium 156mg; Fibre 7.6g; Sodium 211mg

Hungarian Pancakes with Pecan Filling
Pekándiós palacsinta

These light, paper-thin pancakes are filled with pecan nuts and fruit, and are a popular dessert in Hungary. They are usually served rolled or folded into triangles. The pancake recipe can also be used with savoury fillings such as scrambled eggs, mushrooms, seafood and vegetables.

Serves 10–12

115g/4oz/1 cup plain (all-purpose) flour, sifted
pinch of salt
2 eggs
200ml/7fl oz/scant 1 cup milk mixed with 75ml/2$\frac{1}{2}$fl oz/$\frac{1}{3}$ cup water
50g/2oz/$\frac{1}{4}$ cup butter

For the filling

300g/11oz/3$\frac{3}{4}$ cups pecan nuts, roughly chopped
200g/7oz/1 cup caster (superfine) sugar
75ml/5 tbsp single (light) cream
1.5ml/$\frac{1}{4}$ tsp ground cinnamon
45ml/3 tbsp sultanas (golden raisins)
10ml/2 tsp vanilla extract
grated rind of 1 lemon
15ml/1 tbsp apricot jam
30ml/2 tbsp icing (confectioners') sugar

1 Sift the flour and salt into a large bowl, holding the sieve (strainer) high above the bowl to introduce some air. Make a well in the centre of the flour and break the eggs into it. Whisk until smooth.

2 Gradually add small quantities of the milk and water mixture, still whisking. When all the liquid has been added, whisk once more until the batter is smooth and has the consistency of thin cream.

3 Melt the butter in a small frying pan over medium heat. Spoon 30ml/2 tbsp of it into the batter and whisk it in, putting the remaining butter in a bowl to use for cooking the remaining pancakes. Now increase the heat, so that the pan becomes hot, then turn the heat down to medium. Spoon some batter into the pan and tilt the pan so that the batter covers the base. Cook for 1 minute, or until golden and crispy – lift the edge with a palette knife or metal spatula to see if it is tinged gold before turning. Flip the pancake over with a palette knife and cook the other side; it will need only a few seconds.

4 Slide it out of the pan on to a plate. Use the remaining butter and batter to make more pancakes. Stack them as you make them between sheets of baking parchment on a plate over simmering water, to keep them warm while you cook the rest.

5 To make the filling, put the chopped pecan nuts and sugar in a bowl and mix together. Put the cream and the pecan mixture into a pan and cook over medium heat until it becomes the consistency of a thick purée. Remove from the heat.

6 Add the cinnamon, sultanas, vanilla extract, lemon rind and jam, and mix together well. Fill the pancakes with the pecan filling and roll or fold to serve, dusted with a little icing sugar.

PER SERVING: Energy 358kcal/1494kJ; Protein 5g; Carbohydrate 32g, of which sugars 24g; Fat 24g, of which saturates 5g; Cholesterol 53mg; Calcium 66mg; Fibre 0.6g; Sodium 84mg

Hungarian Cherry Strudel
Cseresznyés rétes

Making strudel pastry is a dying art, although in the depths of the countryside, Hungarian women still like to make their own at home – and there's nothing like the real thing. Ready-bought filo pastry is the next best thing, however. A true strudel should be fine, crisp and light, with very thin pastry filled with fruit. Cherries are among the most common fillings for a strudel.

Serves 8

65g/2½oz/5 tbsp butter, melted, plus extra for greasing
750g/1lb 10oz fresh cherries, pitted
15ml/1 tbsp lemon juice
3 cooking apples, cored, peeled and cut into segments
70g/2¾oz/generous ½ cup walnuts, roughly chopped
75g/3oz/6 tbsp caster (superfine) sugar, plus extra for sprinkling
30g/1oz/1½ cups brioche breadcrumbs
60ml/4 tbsp cherry jam
10 large sheets fresh filo pastry, thawed if frozen
caster (superfine) sugar, to sprinkle

COOK'S TIP

It is best to make strudel on a warm day, because the dough can be rolled more easily in a hot room.

1 Preheat the oven to 200°C/400°F/Gas 6. Butter a baking sheet and line with baking parchment. Put the cherries and lemon juice in a pan and cook over medium heat for 2 minutes.

2 In a large bowl, mix together the apples, walnuts, sugar and breadcrumbs. Stir in the cherries. Put the cherry jam in a pan and heat gently until melted.

3 Lay out a damp cloth on the work surface and put a sheet of filo pastry on top (cover the remaining pastry sheets with a damp cloth to stop them from drying out). Brush generously with melted butter, then cover with another sheet of filo, brushing again with butter.

4 Repeat with another sheet of filo pastry, but this time also brush it with melted cherry jam. Repeat the same process with the remaining filo sheets, brushing every third sheet with the cherry jam.

5 Once you have all the filo buttered and stacked in front of you, put the apple, cherry and walnut mixture in the middle of it and roll the pastry up as though it were a Swiss roll (jelly roll).

6 Brush butter over all the sides of the roll, then put on to the prepared tray, seam-side down, with the pastry edge beneath the roll. Sprinkle over some caster sugar and curl into a horseshoe shape. Bake in the preheated oven for 20–30 minutes, until golden brown. Leave to cool on a wire rack.

PER SERVING: Energy 343kcal/1443kJ; Protein 17g; Carbohydrate 44g, of which sugars 38g; Fat 14g, of which saturates 5g; Cholesterol 17mg; Calcium 51mg; Fibre 5.0g; Sodium 147mg

Serves 6

200g/7oz/1 cup pudding rice

400ml/14fl oz/1²/₃ cups double (heavy) cream

750ml/1¹/₄ pints/3 cups full-fat (whole) milk

150g/5oz/³/₄ cup caster (superfine) sugar

15ml/1 tbsp almond extract

3 egg whites

45ml/3 tbsp flaked (sliced) almonds, lightly toasted

Rice and Almond Pudding
Habos-mandulás rizsfelfújt

This is an adaptation of a traditional Hungarian recipe. It is a textural delight, containing the creamy comfort of rice pudding, the luxury of golden meringue tops and the occasional crunchy encounter with toasted almonds, all in all a show-stopping dessert.

1 Preheat the oven to 180°C/350°F/Gas 4. Put the rice and two-thirds of the cream into a heavy pan, and cook over medium heat for 2–3 minutes.

2 Mix well and then add the milk and 30ml/2 tbsp of the sugar. Cook on low heat for another 10–15 minutes, or until the rice grains are soft. When the liquid has more or less evaporated, add the remaining cream and the almond extract.

3 Spoon the egg whites into a clean, grease-free bowl and whisk until they form soft peaks. Whisk in the remaining sugar to make a light meringue.

4 Pour the rice pudding into six individual ovenproof dishes, and either pipe the meringue mixture on top of each pudding, using a piping bag, or just spoon the mixture over.

5 Sprinkle the tops with the almonds. Cook for 8–10 minutes, or until the tops of the meringues are slightly golden in colour.

PER SERVING: Energy 668kcal/2786kJ; Protein 10g; Carbohydrate 62g, of which sugars 33g; Fat 44g, of which saturates 26g; Cholesterol 109mg; Calcium 197mg; Fibre 1.4g; Sodium 103mg

Serves 6–8

12 large sheets fresh filo pastry, thawed
   if frozen
50g/2oz/¹⁄₄ cup butter, melted, plus extra
   for greasing
75ml/5 tbsp ground almonds
10ml/2 tsp poppy seeds
10ml/2 tsp icing (confectioners') sugar

For the filling

60ml/4 tbsp caster (superfine) sugar
60ml/4 tbsp sultanas (golden raisins)
30ml/2 tbsp ground poppy seeds
3 eating apples, peeled and
   thinly sliced

Poppy Seed and Apple Strudel
Mákos-almás rétes

Rétes is the star of Hungarian patisserie – the finest and most delicate of flaky pastry, wrapped around sweet or savoury fillings. Making it from scratch is laborious, but ready-made strudel or filo pastry gives excellent results.

1 To make the filling, put 80–100ml/ 3¹⁄₂fl oz/scant ¹⁄₂ cup water into a pan with the sugar. Bring to the boil and simmer for 2 minutes to dissolve the sugar. Stir in the sultanas and poppy seeds, then set aside to cool. Preheat the oven to 180°C/ 350°F/ Gas 4 and brush a baking sheet with butter.

2 Put the apples in a large mixing bowl and add the cooled sugar syrup, mixing together well. Set aside.

3 Lay a sheet of filo pastry on the prepared baking sheet (cover the remaining sheets with a damp cloth to stop them from drying out). Brush the sheet of filo with melted butter. Sprinkle with some ground almonds. Repeat with another two filo sheets.

4 Spread a thin layer of the apple and poppy seed filling over the filo pastry and then continue with three filo layers as before, followed by another apple and poppy seed layer. Continue until all 12 sheets of filo pastry have been used.

5 Roll up from the short end of the filled pastry layers like a Swiss roll (jelly roll) and tuck in the ends. Turn the strudel seam-side down and brush over all the sides with the remaining butter.

6 Sprinkle with the whole poppy seeds and bake for 25–30 minutes, or until golden brown. Cool completely and dust with icing sugar before serving.

PER SERVING: Energy 420kcal/1764kJ; Protein 34g; Carbohydrate 42g, of which sugars 35g; Fat 26g, of which saturates 7g; Cholesterol 21mg; Calcium 350mg; Fibre 5.2g; Sodium 191mg

Serves 6

10ml/2 tsp butter, melted, for
    greasing
115g/4oz/1 cup pistachio nuts, finely
    chopped
50g/2oz/1 cup brioche breadcrumbs
50g/2oz/¼ cup soft light brown
    sugar
5ml/1 tsp vanilla extract
150ml/¼ pint/⅔ cup double
    (heavy) cream
2 large eggs
500g/1¼lb/3⅓ cups raspberries,
    washed
thick natural (plain) yogurt, to serve

Raspberry and Almond Gratin
Málnás-mandulás szelet

This recipe is from Carmel Pince, possibly the best
Jewish restaurant in Budapest. The dish can also be
prepared with cherries. The use of pistachio nuts is an
Ottoman influence in Hungarian cooking.

1 Preheat the oven to 200°C/400°F/
Gas 6 and lightly butter a 20cm (8in)
medium square cake tin (pan).

2 Put the pistachio nuts, brioche
crumbs, sugar, vanilla, cream and
eggs in a food processor and blend
them until combined. (Alternatively,
beat the eggs, then add to the other
ingredients and stir well.)

3 Spread out the raspberries in one
layer over the base of the cake tin.
Pour in the gratin mixture. Bake for
30 minutes.

4 Leave for 5 minutes to cool in the
tin, then turn out and serve warm,
accompanied by thick natural yogurt.

VARIATIONS
Raspberries make a successful taste
pairing with various other fruits –
including blueberries, blackberries, figs
or peaches. Just add any one of these
fruits in combination with the raspberries
over the base of the cake tin.

PER SERVING: Energy 282kcal/1179kJ; Protein 9g; Carbohydrate 20g, of which sugars 14g; Fat 19g, of which saturates 6g; Cholesterol 100mg; Calcium 75mg; Fibre 6.1g; Sodium 213mg

Makes 20
oil, for greasing
250g/9oz/generous 1 cup cottage cheese
200g/7oz/scant 1 cup curd (farmer's) cheese
5ml/1 tsp ground black pepper
1 large egg yolk
20 sheets filo pastry, thawed if frozen
150g/5oz/10 tbsp butter, melted
30ml/2 tbsp poppy seeds
75–90ml/5–6 tbsp clear honey

Poppy Seed Pastries with Cottage Cheese
Túrós-mákos csomagok

The Hungarians like contrasts in their food, and the combination of salty and sweet is as common as the flavours of sweet and sour. This salty–sweet partnership works best by using creamy home-made cottage cheese, which in this recipe is combined with the natural sweetness of honey. These filo pastries make a perfect breakfast or light dessert.

1 Preheat the oven to 180°C/350°F/ Gas 4 and grease a baking sheet. Combine the cottage cheese and curd cheese in a bowl, then stir in the black pepper and egg yolk.

2 Take a sheet of filo pastry and cover the remaining pastry sheets with a damp cloth. Lightly brush the sheet of filo with some melted butter and fold in half lengthways. Brush with butter and fold it in half again.

3 Put some cheese mixture on the pastry along the shorter edge and roll the pastry over the filling away from you to form a small Swiss roll (jelly roll). Make sure you fold the sides of the pastry inward at the same time, to enclose the filling. Do not roll too tightly. Put on to the baking sheet. Continue with the remaining filo sheets and cheese mixture.

4 Brush the pastries with melted butter, then sprinkle with poppy seeds. Bake in the oven for 20 minutes, or until golden brown. Serve warm with a little honey to drizzle over the pastry.

PER SERVING: Energy 101kcal/428kJ; Protein 15g; Carbohydrate 8g, of which sugars 6g; Fat 3g, of which saturates 1g; Cholesterol 15mg; Calcium 63mg; Fibre 0.5g; Sodium 118mg

Hungarian Chocolate Almond Torte
Mandulás csokoládétorta

This cake is inspired by the rich and delectable tortes served in the little Café Ruszwurm in Budapest, which is easily the best place to have classic Hungarian cakes and pastries. This is a light and devilishly moreish cake.

Serves 10–12

150g/5oz/10 tbsp butter, plus extra
  for greasing
200g/7oz dark (bittersweet) chocolate
  (containing 70% cocoa solids), chopped
6 large eggs, separated
150g/5oz/⅔ cup soft light brown sugar
30ml/2 tbsp plain (all-purpose) flour
115g/4oz/1 cup ground almonds

For the ganache
150ml/¼ pint/⅔ cup double (heavy) cream
200g/7oz dark (bittersweet) chocolate
  (containing 70% cocoa solids), chopped

For the almond topping
150g/5oz/¾ cup caster (superfine) sugar
200g/7oz/1¾ cups flaked (sliced)
  almonds, roasted

COOK'S TIP
• Chopping chocolate helps it melt more quickly – dark chocolate is best divided into nut-size pieces.
• To avoid scorching the chocolate, put it in a heatproof bowl and put this in a shallow pan filled with hot water. Keep stirring it so that it melts evenly.

1 Preheat the oven to 180°C/350°F/Gas 4. Grease and line a 20cm/8in round cake tin (pan), and line it with baking parchment. Melt the butter very slowly over low heat. Remove from the heat and add the chopped chocolate, stirring constantly so that it melts in the hot butter. Leave to cool.

2 In a large bowl, whisk the egg yolks and sugar together until thick and pale. Add the chocolate mixture and mix well. Sift in the flour and ground almonds, and carefully mix together.

3 Put the egg whites into a clean, grease-free bowl and whisk until they form soft peaks. Fold the egg whites carefully into the mixture to retain as much air as possible in the batter.

4 Pour into the prepared tin and bake for 25 minutes. The cake will be set but slightly wobbly in the centre. Leave to cool in the tin.

5 To make the ganache, heat the cream to almost boiling point. Immediately remove from the heat and add the chopped chocolate. Stir until all of it is amalgamated. Cool and then pour over the cake to glaze. Leave to set.

6 To make the almond topping, lightly oil a sheet of baking parchment. Put the sugar and 100ml/3½fl oz/scant ½ cup water in a pan and cook until lightly caramelized. Remove from the heat and add the flaked almonds. Stir briefly to coat.

7 Using tongs, and working quickly, take out small clusters of the sticky nuts and put on the baking parchment to cool. Top the cake with the almond clusters and serve.

PER SERVING: Energy 636kcal/2653kJ; Protein 12g; Carbohydrate 51g, of which sugars 48g; Fat 45g, of which saturates 18g; Cholesterol 176mg; Calcium 113mg; Fibre 3.5g; Sodium 135mg

Serves 8

150g/5oz/10 tbsp soft butter, plus extra
　for greasing
150g/5oz/¾ cup caster (superfine) sugar
4 eggs, separated
150g/5oz plain (all-purpose) flour
5ml/1 tsp baking powder
50g/2oz ground almonds
500g/1¼lb/3⅓ cups fresh cherries, pitted
5ml/1 tsp almond extract
15–30ml/1–2 tbsp flaked (sliced) almonds

Cherry and Almond Cake
Cseresznyés-mandulás pite

This favourite home-made cake is easy to make. Cherries and almonds are well
established as compatible partners in desserts. This dish, however, tastes just as good
using plums, apricots or other soft fruits as with sweet and juicy cherries.

1 Preheat the oven to 180°C/350°F/
Gas 4 and butter a 25 x 15cm/10 x 6in
baking tray. Put the butter and sugar in
a bowl and beat until light and creamy.

2 Beat in the egg yolks one by one,
adding a spoonful of sifted flour and
a spoonful of baking powder between
each one. Sift over the remaining flour
and baking powder, and fold into the
egg and butter. Stir in the almonds.

3 Put the egg whites into a clean,
grease-free bowl and whisk until they
form stiff peaks. Fold the egg whites
gently into the mixture to retain as
much air as possible in the batter.
Do not overmix.

4 Put the pitted cherries in a bowl
and add the almond extract. Mix
to combine. Sprinkle the almond
cherries over the base of the
baking tray. Pour the cake batter
over the top.

5 Sprinkle with the flaked almonds
and bake for 30–35 minutes, or until
golden. Cool completely and cut into
squares to serve.

PER SERVING: Energy 349kcal/1459kJ; Protein 4g; Carbohydrate 42g, of which sugars 28g; Fat 19g, of which saturates 10g; Cholesterol 40mg; Calcium 61mg; Fibre 2.5g; Sodium 176mg

Serves 8

300g/11oz shortcrust pastry, thawed if
    frozen
flour, for dusting
1 egg yolk, beaten
15ml/1 tbsp icing (confectioners') sugar

For the walnut filling

300g/11oz/2³/₄ cups walnuts, roughly
    chopped
200g/7oz/1 cup caster (superfine) sugar
75ml/5 tbsp single (light) cream
1.5ml/¹/₄ tsp ground cinnamon
45ml/3 tbsp raisins
10ml/2 tsp vanilla extract
grated rind of 1 lemon
15ml/1 tbsp orange marmalade

Hungarian Christmas Loaf
Beigli

This is a loaf that every Hungarian family will prepare for the Christmas celebrations. It is a little like a strudel but is instead made with shortcrust pastry. Walnuts and dried fruits are always used for the filling.

1 Preheat the oven to 180°C/350°F/ Gas 4 and line a baking sheet with baking parchment. To make the walnut filling, put the chopped walnuts and sugar into a bowl and mix together well.

2 Put the cream and the walnut mixture into a pan and cook over medium heat until it becomes the consistency of a thick purée.

3 Remove from the heat. Add the cinnamon, raisins, vanilla extract, lemon rind and marmalade and mix.

4 Roll out the pastry on a floured board to a large rectangle about 3mm/¹/₈in thick.

5 Spread the walnut filling over the rectangle, leaving a border of 1cm/¹/₂in around the edges.

6 Roll up the dough sheet, starting from the longer side, then lay it seam-side down on the baking sheet. Brush with the egg yolk and bake for 15–20 minutes, or until golden brown. Cool completely and sprinkle with icing sugar before serving.

PER SERVING: Energy 584kcal/2437kJ; Protein 9g; Carbohydrate 54g, of which sugars 36g; Fat 39g, of which saturates 7g; Cholesterol 36mg; Calcium 87mg; Fibre 5.2g; Sodium 191mg

Useful addresses

AUSTRALIA

Audrey & Marco
PO Box 371, Edgecliff NSW 2027
T: (02) 8356 9773
www.audreyandmarco.com.au
Gourmet delicatessen

Balkan Smallgoods
339–341 Springvale Road,
3171, Springvale, Victoria
T: (03) 9546 5023
mrakidzi@bigpond.com.au
Meat and general groceries

CANADA

Budapest Delicatessen Ltd
9308 111 Avenue, Edmonton,
Alberta
www.budapestdeli.ca

Bank Street Sausage & Deli
1920 Bank Street, Ottawa,
Ontario ON K1V 7Z8
www.banksausagedeli.com/
index.html

Blue Danube Sausage House
24 Chauncey Ave. Etobicoke,
Ontario, ON, M8Z 2Z4
www.bluedanubesausagehouse.
com
Smokehouse and delicatessen

**Hungarian Honey Bear
Delicatessen**
249 Sheppard Avenue East
Toronto, Ontario M2N 3A8
T: (+1) 416 733 0022
mezesmacko@hotmail.com
www.mezesmacko.com

Mak European Delicatessens
1335 Lawrence Ave East,
Toronto, Ontario, ON, M3A 1C6
www.makdeli.com

HUNGARY

Angelika Cafe & Restaurant
Batthyány tér 7, I. District
Budapest
Café and restaurant

Gerbeaud Coffee House
Café Gerbeaud
Vörösmarty tér 7
Budapest 1051
T: 00-36-1-419-9020

Great Market Hall
Fovám tér, Pest end of Liberty
Bridge, Budapest
Fruit, vegetables and groceries

Ruszwurm Coffee House
Szentháromság utca 7,
Castle District, Budapest

Taste Hungary
Jégverem utca 6
Budapest, 1011
T: +36-20-453-6095
hello@tastehungary.com
Food, wine and market tours

UK

Baltic Branch
Queen Street, Argyle Centre
Ramsgate CT11 9EE
T: +44 (0)1843 582829
East European food

Daiva's Shop
25b Abbotsbury Road
Morden
London SM4 5LJ
info@daivashop.co.uk
T: +44 (0)7868 847554
East European food and drinks

Hungarian Delicatessen
Magyarok Boltja Londonban
52 Sewardstone Road
London E4 7PR
hungapol@btinternet.com
www.hungapol.webs.com

Hungarian Food Centre
430 Finchley Road
London NW2 2HY
T: +44 (0)20 7431 8205

Hungarian Food Market
28 Acregate Lane
Preston PR1 5QN
T: +44 (0)7860 934161
www.hungarianfoodmarket.co.uk

**Roman Delicatessen
Merchants Ltd**
112 Churchfield Road
London W3 6BY
T: +44 (0)20 8992 2055
www.romandeli.co.uk
Meats, salads and fish

USA

**Andre's Hungarian Strudels &
Pastries**
100-28 Queens Blvd, Forest Hills
New York NY 11375
www.andresbakery.com
Strudels and pastries

Bende Inc.
925 Corporate Woods Pkwy,
Vernon Hills, Illinois IL 60061
www.bende.com
Groceries and meats

Budapest Deli
10307 Vassar Ave, Chatsworth
California, CA 91311
quickshipeurope.com

Budapest Market
6380 . S. Eastern Ave Unit 6,
Las Vegas, Nevada NV 89120
quickshipeurope.com

City Fresh Market
3201 W. Devon Ave., Chicago,
IL 60659
T: (773) 681-8600
www.cityfreshmarket.com

Continent Deli
4150 Regents Park Row, #110,
La Jolla, CA
T: (858) 623-0099

**Dettcris Hungarian
Delicatessen**
6250 N Federal Hwy, Florida
FL 33308
www.dettcris.com

efooddepot.com
7505 N. Broadway Extension #A
Oklahoma City, Oklahoma 73116
T: (888) 553-5650
www.efooddepot.com
Worldwide mail order

Hungarian Bakery
1240 Templeton Circle,
Earlysville, Virginia VA 22936
www.hungarianbakery.com

Hungarian Delicious
T: +36 21 202 1481
www.hungariandelicious.com
*Mail order for USA, Canada,
Australia and New Zealand*

Hungarian Kosher Foods
4020 Oakton St
(between Crawford Ave &
Keystone Ave), Skokie, IL 60076
T: (847) 674-8008

Hungarian Meats & Deli
311 Somerset St, New
Brunswick, New Jersey NJ 08901
www.hungarianmeatsanddeli.com

International Meat & Deli
10382 Stanford Ave, Garden
Grove, California, CA
intlmeatanddeli.com

**Tulipán Hungarian Pastry and
Coffee Shop**
122 S. Market St., Wooster
Ohio, OH 44691
www.tulipanhungarianpastry.com

Yorkville Meat Emporium
1560 2nd Ave
New York, NY 10028
www.hungarianmeatmarket.com

ZABAR'S
2245 Broadway (at 80th St.),
New York, NY 10024
T: (800) 697-6301 or (212) 496-
1234 (NYC)
www.zabars.com

Index